Weaponize Your Mental Game by Unlocking

# God's Sports Arsenal

by

Steven M. Leonard

Copyright © 2020 by Steven M. Leonard
ISBN 978-0-9982281-1-2

The first edition all rights reserved. No portion of this book may be reproduced, stored in a retrieval system, or transmitted in any form or by any means—electronic, mechanical, photocopy, recording, scanning, or any other—except for brief quotations in critical reviews or articles, without prior written permission of the publisher.

Trace Mountain Media
129 S. Phelps Ave. Ste 206
Rockford, IL 61108
Website: GodsSportsArsenal.com

All scripture quotations, unless otherwise indicated, are taken from the Holy Bible, New International Version®, NIV®. Copyright ©1973, 1978, 1984, 2011 by Biblica, Inc. ™ Used by permission of Zondervan. All rights reserved worldwide. www.zondervan.com The "NIV" and "New International Version" are trademarks registered in the United States Patent and Trademark Office by Biblica, Inc.™

Scripture quotations marked (ESV) are from The Holy Bible, English Standard Version® (ESV®), copyright ©2001 by Crossway, a publishing ministry of Good News Publishers. Used by permission. All rights reserved.

Scripture quotations marked (GNT) are taken from Good News Translation Copyright © 1992 by the American Bible Society.

Scripture quotations marked WEB are taken from the *World English Bible.*

The cover design depicts the Coliseum in Rome. It was famous for the numerous sporting events and a place where many Christians died because of their faith.

Version 7.1

***Printed in the United States of America***

**Throughout history, all types of warriors have searched for ways to prepare their minds for the coming battle:**

- ***Biblical warriors*** **who fought for their lives**
- ***Professional sports warriors***
- **Even today's** ***weekend warriors***

**All such warriors seek the unwavering confidence and courage that come from mental preparation. Some call this process, "putting on your game face."**

**When Goliath-sized doubts have the power to hold you back, you are engaging in spiritual warfare. These situations require God's help. Fear not. God has a game plan to destroy paralyzing doubts by using weapons from his arsenal. The weapons you will receive have divine power to restore your courage to fight and talent to conquer.**

## Legal Disclaimer

**Before beginning this or any other type of self-improvement program, please consult a duly qualified doctor, therapist, or coach. The instruction presented herein is *not* intended to be a substitute for the guidance of any healthcare or sports professional.**

**Competing in sports can be dangerous. Training for competitive sports can be just as dangerous. Injuries, even career-ending injuries, do occur regardless of proper mental training. Though we cannot eliminate risk, we can minimize it by always following the rule book, wearing proper safety equipment, and using the proper techniques under the supervision of certified trainers and coaches. You should not use any of the ideas in this book to enhance performance without the express approval of a certified trainer and/or coach. Neither the author nor the publisher shall be liable for any injuries that result from following the guidance in this book.**

# God's Sports Arsenal

# Chapter Read-Times



**Total reading time: 5 hours 38 minutes**

# Introduction

When you come from a small town, the gene pool for football athletes is limited. My height and average sports talent made me a good fit to play tight end.

Good coaches were hard to find, too. The history teacher looked like a football player, so the administration must have decided he would make a good head coach.

During one scrimmage, our head coach was frustrated with the offensive line's sloppy blocking. So he grabbed a lineman for a teaching moment. Speaking loud enough for the team to hear, he said, "We are going to hand you the ball, and nobody will block ... so you can see what it feels like."

That scrawny, 150-pound lineman suddenly found some serious motivation. Taking the handoff, he bolted like a spooked donkey that no one could stop and dragged the entire defensive unit for 10 yards.

Our shocked coach said, "OK, today we are going to make you a running back!"

Finding that "something extra" to make a game-changing difference proved an elusive search for me. Throughout my four years of high school football, I played one great game—only one. It came during my junior year, and I was never able to duplicate that performance.

I always blamed my lack of consistency on the coaching staff. Yet, I also noticed that even extremely talented players in the NFL with great coaches still found ways to choke.

My coach wasn't the problem: *I* was the problem. But how, in that one great game, did I stumble upon excellence? What is the secret to executing superior performance?

Thus began my journey for answers. Since then, I've been studying professional athletes by reading about their battles with mental preparation and performance anxiety. My decades-long search also took me to other fonts of wisdom, including the practical advice found in the Bible.

In this book, I share the best solutions I have found to deal with the uniqueness of the competitive mind. Please read on.

# God's Sports Arsenal

# Game Within the Game

## Chapter 1

In sports, words are powerful weapons. When athletes are equipped with extreme emotion, their words are armed to intimidate hearts and minds. Superstar athletes routinely fire off verbal bullets aimed at wounding a competitor's mental game. Fans, triggered with hostility can be just as combative and twice as loud. These "guardians of the bleachers" wear painted faces, wedged-shaped cheese helmets, and other outlandish battle-gear. These dedicated fans love to line up along the visiting team's tunnel to get inside a rival's head. They hurl word grenades filled with hate and defeatisms to destroy a competitor's confidence.

But could it be that easy to hit a nerve and paralyze a professional athlete's performance? Can such spirited taunting shoot down the mental game, or do some pros have multi-threat resistant body armor to survive the bombardment of never-ending verbal attacks?

Trash-talk has always been a part of the "game within the game." However, there was a time when the exchange of word grenades was, at worst, annoying and didn't threaten to physically end an opposing athlete's career.

Yogi Berra, Hall of Fame catcher for the New York Yankees, was known for his non-stop trash-talk. He would stand behind home plate and start jawing as soon as the batter stepped into the batter's box. A story has it that Hank Aaron, the home run champion of his time and the first to break Babe Ruth's record, got quite an earful from Yogi one day. "You're holding the bat wrong; you're holding the bat wrong," Yogi scolded. "You're supposed to be able to read the trademark; you're supposed to be able to read the trademark." When Arron clobbered the next pitch into the left field bleachers, he turned to Yogi and said, "I didn't come here to read!"

Another famous Yogi quote is "90% of the game is half mental." Though I still scratch my head about his math, his point is powerful: The mental aspect of sports is massive.

I studied the impact of taunting from superstars in the years before the NFL imposed penalties for unsportsmanlike behavior. More than half the time, the football team with the biggest mouth would get clobbered. When trash-talk is a big part of the mental game it sometimes backfires. It can make a weaker team boiling mad, motivating them to succeed if for no other reason than to embarrass the loud-mouth athlete and shut down their fans.

Even without the motivation of trash-talk, good teams can struggle to be consistent. They fly high one week only to crash and burn the next. The powerhouse teams that win the Super Bowl often suffer from the jinx of not making the playoffs the following year.

What is this mystery of the mind that has frustrated competitors in every game and every sport? What motivates one team to excel, and what paralyzes another? These questions baffle coaches, athletes, and die-hard fans. A few great athletes have cracked the code to improve their mental game, while others are clueless about how this mysterious "something extra" comes and goes so quickly during the game.

When Yogi tried to take away Hank's "something extra," he didn't have a clue that trash-talk would trigger the confidence and skills for a home run. Could there be a simple explanation why some athletes are inspired to be winners and others are jinxed with losing?

As it turns out, the secret to staying on top of your game is not that complicated. A championship performance is achieved when your mental game is focused on speeding up your reaction time. That means you must find that "something extra" to turbo-charge your motor neurons. In turn, these revved-up motor neurons will rev up your performance. Your competitive edge shows up when your mind-muscle connections can operate at lightning-fast speeds.

The challenge lies, not only in motivating your motor neurons, but in building pathways that allow them to hit game speed. If you make the necessary connections, your thought process can call for high-octane action, and these pathways become short-cuts to your skillset. The more pathways that are activated during your pre-game program, the faster you can read and react to game situations. Thus, gaining an advantage by consistently keeping your brain and brawn in sync.

Your mental game is a "game within the game" that takes place before and during a competitive event. Setting goals, visualizing those goals, and using extreme repetition are ways to ramp-up your skill set, but that's just the starting line. We will be enhancing these fundamental mind-games and installing performance-enhancing upgrades to have you consistently hitting on all cylinders.

Before you know it, your motor neurons will be revved-up with maximum horsepower, plus your mental pathways will be transformed into lightning-fast expressways. When that happens, everyone knows what it looks like. Your new level of performance will be described as *unstoppable*, *on fire*, or *in the zone*.

In the real world, the textbook term for a mental connection is "learned association." Your neurons and pathways allow us to set up a network of "mental reminders" to use in our daily lives. For example, seeing a red light means stop, so the connection is made for your right foot to hit the brake. And, a green light means go, so you step on the gas pedal. If you make the mistake of adding an emotional connection to your driving skills, your thoughts are upgraded, weaponized with road rage.

## Chapter 1

An enjoyable emotional connection can be the smell of warm homemade cookies and the desire to dunk them in a glass of cold milk, which also links the entire experience to a smorgasbord of favorite comfort foods.

A longtime friend of mine once told his friends that his parents were dropping by for a short visit. He warned his friends not to mention his parents' size because they were really tall and sensitive about their height. When his parents arrived, they were very small and short. My buddy enjoyed watching his friends fight back the urge to laugh out loud.

My friend had played with the mental connections found in making a first impression. Meeting someone for the first time triggers the process of taking mental snapshots and tagging general info to those new images. My friend the jokester, had prepared his friends to see tall people. When the opposite happened, his parents' appearance triggered a potentially embarrassing situation.

Making everyday mental connections is relatively easy. Generally, 90% of our thoughts are repetitive because we have already labeled the information and emotions for various situations. When daily life is compared to competitive sports, it's a whole new ball game. Judging the distance for a nothing-but-net 3-pointer, or calculating the point of impact when facing a 90+ mph fastball is a lot more challenging. What about making an emotional connection, as in maintaining the confidence to close out the final 2-minutes of a close game? These skills, found in many championship athletes, are considered to be un-coachable. Their natural talent is said to be a part of their DNA, but as we will see, these mysteries of the competitive mind are not as difficult as they sound.

The easiest way to understand this game within the game is to see how some of the greatest pro athletes set themselves up for victory. The human mind is indeed complex, so each athlete has a different approach when it comes to mental preparation. Yet, when we analyze how pro athletes set up a battle-zone between the ears, several common strategies emerge.

When it comes to the prep work for your next game, how well do your mind-games stack up to the top athletes in the world? Is your current program similar to the mindset of LeBron James, Tiger Woods, and Jerry Rice? Maybe your pre-game program shares a common bond with Mike Singletary and Michael Jordan. Or perhaps your pre-game strategy better aligns with such top-tier great athletes as Michael Phelps, Walter Payton, or Shaquille O'Neal.

If "none of the above" or "can I use a lifeline?" is your final answer, then perhaps your mental game depends on lucky clothing or a ritual to provide that "something extra." If that is the case you're not alone, many sports celebrities have a superstitious nature.

Before Super Bowl 41, former Chicago Bears middle linebacker Brian Urlacher took a mental chill-pill. Instead of running tackling drills through his mind, his game-day ritual involved kicking back and spending an hour watching his favorite fishing show. Once at the stadium, he listened to music and ate two chocolate chip cookies (his comfort food) before putting on his game face.

Jim Leyland, the manager of the Detroit Tigers, made my "Top 10 Mojo List" with his devotion to luck. Leyland earns high honors by not changing his underwear when winning baseball games. Even when the Tigers ran off a 12-game winning streak in 2011, he continued to wear the same pair of undies. Leyland doesn't stop there. To take the top spot among the superstitious, however, requires a custom mix of aromatherapy. Leyland enjoys a pre-game ritual of puffing a lucky smelly cigar to join forces with the power of his lucky fragrant underwear.

Other celebrities on the superstitious list include a tennis player who ties her shoes a certain way and won't change her socks during a tournament when winning; a football player who requires a slap in the face before games; a coach who eats the grass to be a part of the football field; golfers who kiss the ball before every putt; and a baseball player who sleeps with his lucky bat to continue a hot streak. Even the ritual of giving the head coach a congratulatory Gatorade-ice bath, which started as a prank by players who disliked their coach, was continued because it was thought to bring good luck in the next game.

Looking to spark some game-time motivation is not all bad, even for unpaid athletes. Several studies have examined the link between luck and improved athletic performance. In one study, students were told they were using a golf ball that had proved to be lucky. They consistently sank more putts than students who were not given inside information about its special powers.

Even though superstitious rituals and lucky charms are little-known secrets of professional athletes, the association with sports doesn't offer a strong connection—not enough to consistently improve your mental game. If the human condition is indeed wired to believe in that "something extra," doesn't it make sense to believe in something more powerful than alleged lucky golf balls, stinky cigars, and dirty underwear?

## The NBA's Loaded Gun

One of the big names in pro basketball (at least for now) is LeBron James or, as his close friends call him, "King James." LeBron made a name for himself playing for the Cleveland Cavaliers. His quest to become royalty and be adorned with championship bling led him to the Miami Heat. After spending four years in Miami and winning two NBA championships, he followed his heart and returned home. His dream of rebuilding the Cavaliers into a championship team became a reality in 2016. In a history-making seven game series, the Cavs became the first NBA team to overcome a 3-1 deficit to win a world championship.

Early in LeBron's pro career his popularity grew quickly. His picture soon graced the cover of *USA Weekend*, which labeled him "already arguably the #1 basketball player on the planet." The news show *60 Minutes* invited him to appear and talk about his well-known skills in mentally preparing for big games. During the broadcast, the interviewer asked, "What is your most powerful weapon on the basketball court?"

I expected him to cite one of his many offensive skills, such as his ball-handling or scoring ability beyond the three-point line. His unpredictable reply was, "My mind is my most powerful weapon!" My ears stood at attention when I heard a concept, I could believe in. LeBron's "game within the game" centers around a military connection. When he steps onto the basketball court, he is at war. Somehow, he has learned to associate his competitive experience with a battlefield. His mental prep has weaponized his thoughts with emotion and triggered the feeling of being armed and dangerous.

How does LeBron load his most powerful weapon—his mind? By connecting his thoughts to a word picture. Lebron has a mental image of rival athletes that prove threatening. He then sets up predictable scoring opportunities, which translates into the mental connections needed to neutralize his opponent's game. These descriptive tags never leave his mind but become the ammo for a military advantage.

Though fans don't realize it, they follow a similar line of thinking. They will also gather info about an athlete and create a sports related word picture. Not only do fans attach a name tag, jersey number, and physical features to this mental snapshot, but also a perception of their talent. This tagging process can also transform a fan's competitive attitude. They can end up cheering their hearts out for the home-town athletes, then launch loud and abusive word grenades to disrupt a competitor's confidence.

# Chapter 1

If you could hold one of LeBron's sports thoughts in your hand, you would notice an upgraded 2.0 version of this tagging process. This type of mental activity is also similar to the first-impression process, only LeBron's mental picture of his adversary connects with more motor neurons. You would also see numerous tags filled with aggressiveness to combat his rival's skills and weaknesses. The high volume of tags provides a competitive edge for LeBron to stay in the zone regardless of the situation. These performance-enhancing tags have now become *sports tags*.

If a sports tag is done correctly, thoughts are weaponized by adding an emotional boost to give you a competitive advantage. These tags have the power to motivate your entire sports psyche with a high level of game-time emotion and initialize fundamental skills. When you combine logic with unwavering confidence, your thoughts are *weaponized* with emotion to trigger an explosive transformation in athletic performance.

When LeBron uses sports tags as ammo, his most powerful weapon—his mind, is upgraded to a "weapon of confidence." He can take over a game because he has set up his mental game. He knows exactly what to do, which gives him the confidence to shoot down any opposing athlete's strengths. When LeBron targets his weaponized thoughts and pulls the trigger, watch the fun begin as he blows-up his opponent's game.

If you can relate to a military mindset, just the thought of having a new weapon to use during games will assure an attitude adjustment. The X's and O's from the playbook will now become combat scenarios you need to complete your mission. Whether you realize it or not, by taking time to strategize, you're also weaponizing an emotional part of the game—confidence. Anytime you use an underlying story to make your combat scenarios come to life, the combination of logic and emotion triggers a sense of danger and exhilaration in your game.

Later, we will be covering the Armor of God and other spiritual weapons, but what if you can't relate to a military mindset? What if weaponizing your thoughts and taking thoughts captive sounds offensive due to a personal experience with gun violence or your beliefs about military conflicts? Then it's time to modify the symbolism needed to improve your sports psyche. Your mental game is just that, a game, so adapt to a new game. How about switching from a loaded weapon to a loaded deck of cards? Playing the "confidence card" can be just as effective as possessing a "weapon of confidence." When you analyze your opponent's weaknesses, playing the "one better card" can give you the confidence and competitive advantage to neutralize your rival's performance.

Warning! As you load your mind to make use of sports tags, beware of overconfidence! Replacing pre-game strategies with superhero fantasies will create a pretentious weapon of confidence or a useless wild card. Your mental game can become your greatest strength, but if you're not careful, your greatest vulnerability. An arrogant attitude can make you feel invincible which results in rookie decisions or ill-advised plays. A self-serving ego can also get you into major foul trouble or result in a strike-out by trying to kill the ball. To safely handle your new sports weapon or deal out a loaded deck of cards, you need specialized training.

## Sports Rules of Engagement

My twin sons are 6 feet 2 inches now, but they started playing soccer when they were only knee-high. Since the team needed a coach, I volunteered. Halfway through the season, the innocent mini athletes huddled up before a big game. Thinking I should talk on their level and motivate them to put on their game faces, I got down on my knees. It was hard not to smile when all the moms had ribbed them as "so cute in their baggy uniforms." The best I could do was explain that we were undefeated, and today we would be playing the only other undefeated team. I was startled when they began chanting "Kill, kill, kill!" and punching the air overhead with a dozen small fists.

Having never played on, much less *coached*, a soccer team before, I had no idea what was going on. My first thought was, "This is awesome! These guys are on fire!" Then I wondered where that "kill them all" attitude came from and how it would affect their performance. Once the reality of the situation started to sink in, I stopped them and said, "Hold up, nobody is killing anyone today, unless it's the ball. You can attack the ball and kill *it!*" That is exactly what they did. Even our weakest players showed no respect for the other team's talent. Our micro-warriors fearlessly challenged their star opponents, and in the end, we did kill them on the scoreboard.

From a coaching perspective, seeing athletes filled with that much energy and emotion before game time is great. A team's competitive passion can motivate them to be much more than the sum of the individual players. But their efforts to load and fire an effective sports tag needed some tweaking. My coaching instructions needed to clarify what it takes to win, and the emotional part of their tag was misdirected, so it crossed the line. That was not what we had practiced to stay in the zone of aggressiveness, but it was still usable.

If the team had continued to focus their killing mentality on opposing players, we would have lost our competitive edge. That is because their sports tag was aimed at the wrong target. At their age, the ball needed to be the target of their aggression. That way, when the opportunity arose, the ball would trigger a transformation in athletic performance. By redirecting their aim to kill the ball—even our weakest player, who was often distracted by passing butterflies, couldn't wait to fearlessly attack the ball with total disregard for a competitor's strength or talent.

This pre-game ceremony of chanting and fist-bumping ignored a vital rule when trying to weaponize your mental game:

***Target what matters most.***

When this directive is broken, athletes lose their laser focus. Game-winning priorities are overrun by distractions, so expect to see rookie mistakes that end in penalties, such as unsportsmanlike conduct, or missed scoring opportunities that would win a close game.

In my study of pro athletes, several pre-game strategies emerged. Two of the distinct styles were miles apart. At one extreme are athletes who's thought process was dominated by the logical aspect of the game. Like LeBron, their "game within the game" is about finding a strategic advantage. They are playing futuristic *head* games to establish greatness. At the other extreme are athletes who live for the emotional part of the game. They must follow the *heart* and depend on its competitive passion to drive them to a championship performance.

Most athletes are not sure which direction to take or even know about the various pathways to greatness. Unless that unpredictable "something extra" shows up with some type of inspiration, they are depending on luck to take the wheel. Why trust your destiny to the power of luck when the truth is obvious?

***Achieving anything of great value will require utilizing the specialized talents in one's head and heart.***

As you might have guessed, your heart and its underlings of motor neurons, require emotion as their "something extra." Emotion is the nitro-fuel they need to hit top speed.

In the same context, one's head and its followers need to be surrounded by logic to reach new heights. In either case, anytime you strategize and can visualize yourself executing the game plan, it sets up the pathways to greatness. If you're hesitant to believe that different parts of your sports psyche have to combine their efforts to reach a championship level of performance, then it's time to examine the "Greatest Commandment" in the Bible. It appears in Mark 12:30.

> ***Love the Lord your God with all your heart and with all your soul and with all your mind and with all your strength.***

Achieving greatness in God's eyes requires more than physical skills. It involves utilizing the unique strengths of your heart, mind, and even your *soul*. All throughout the Bible, hundreds of verses acknowledge the benefits and detriments of these powerful entities. We see ourselves as individuals, but from God's perspective, your ability to make a difference is determined by the sum of your multiple talents. It will take all three of you to achieve the greatest of God's Commandments.

If this is a new perspective, then you are facing a new challenge. Coming up with a mental game to target greatness might sound like a formidable request, but when factoring in a biblical perspective, you're aiming to unite the strengths of the heart, and mind, and go deep within your soul. God's request for greatness also calls for unifying the passion of your individual entities with one singular and powerful emotion—love.

When it comes to sports, what is the pathway to greatness? Let's start by transforming the head and heart to a game-ready status by connecting these two entities. If you can motivate them to team up, they can boost your intensity. Strategizing, and citing a list of statistics might excite the mind, but it's not the total package. Convincing the heart to excel requires profound emotion in the form of a story. This objective can only be completed if your descriptive sports tags become a part of the narrative.

For example, the storyline in a movie must do a convincing job of tagging the villain as evil, before an attitude adjustment takes place. The hearts and minds of the audience are taken on an emotional journey where they end up hating the bad guy and feel compassion towards his victim. Of course, an unlikely hero has to show up to save the day before the heart and mind can enjoy a predictable happy ending.

To transform into a sports warrior, is it better for your pre-game narrative to focus on the head or the heart? In other words, is it better to energize the heart with emotion or develop the mind's analytical expertise? Absolutely! There is no easy answer when your sports psyche requires the skills and teamwork from both to trigger a stellar performance.

Regrettably, the head and heart relationship is not without speed bumps. The head and even more so the heart have such strong thoughts and desires; it's as if two micro-warriors are competing to drive one sports body.

At times, you can be your own worst enemy or your toughest competitor. So when mistakes happen during a game, an internal conflict is inevitable. In that moment, you are at war with two sides of yourself or biblically speaking, a "double minded man." (James 1:8) The inner sense of strength and confidence is lost only to be replaced by a finger-pointing clash of petty blame and frustration. When either the head or heart has a major meltdown, it paralyzes your future performance and if extreme, the indecision guarantees a spot on the bench.

When it comes to leadership skills, will it be the head or the heart that steps forward to take charge? Executing your best game ever is not always about "who's the best"—but who will drag you down? Will your analytical *mind* hesitate to pull the trigger because of overthinking too many details, or will your *heart* be overcome by the fear of losing control in the final minutes of a close game?

With two fierce competitors like this, it doesn't matter who's in charge if it ends up being a positive working relationship. Just because LeBron cooks up a pre-game program that is stuck spinning around inside his *head* doesn't mean his *heart* isn't up to speed and adding extra ingredients. It underwrites all his sports strategies with a king-sized portion of adrenal energy. The sports tags that label his opponent's tendencies and weaknesses also contain the emotional energy to neutralize his rival's strengths. In the end, LeBron's head is prepared to play an intelligent game and his heart is energized with extreme confidence.

Now you know why a "weapon of confidence" can be one of the most valuable firearms in your arsenal. When loaded with the right ammo—sports tags, it's ready to fire the dynamic duo of logic and emotion. Likewise, a "confidence card" has universal appeal. When either weapon of choice is done right, it can inspire the competitive passion of the heart and mind. Now both mindsets can work towards a common goal and supply you with game-time superpowers.

## Loading Verbal Confidence

To play at LeBron's level involves taking a giant step up in mental preparation. Before taking an enormous leap to feel armed and dangerous during games, work on your social game. Practice firing your weapon or card of confidence while in the real world.

Let's face it, guys. You may dress to impress, but the majority of men tend to be passive in social situations. You spend little time and effort filling your bag of tricks with verbal confidence. Instead of sitting on the sidelines and playing the role of an introvert, why not step out of your comfort zone, take control of the upcoming event and have some fun?

As mentioned, words are powerful weapons. When loaded with extreme emotion they can be a game changer. What about changing hearts and minds by inspiring others with humor? It's a short story loaded with emotion, but can it trigger a transformation in people's hearts and minds? Almost instantaneously!

At your next gathering of friends or family, set the tone by weaponizing your words with humor. Don't accept moments of awkward silence. Have your weapon or card of confidence fully loaded, ready to fire off a humorous ice-breaker. When the conversation starts with "What have you been up to?" or "How are you?" don't repeat the same old no-brainer answer of "Nothing" or "Good." These one-word answers make some noise, but like firing blanks, they have no verbal impact. Instead, anticipate this question and arm yourself with some fresh vocal ammo that packs a bigger punch.

Before your next social event, prepare some comical one-liners that answer the predictable "How are you?" question. Instead of muttering a tired "Doing okay," amp it up with "I can't contain my happiness; I'm out on parole or I just had my ankle monitor removed" You could also try, "I am living the American dream ... out of a cardboard box." Acknowledge a married couple by announcing, "The Beauty and the Beast have arrived." If someone is having a bad day, ask, "Did you get kicked out of the Happiness Club?" If someone is filled with exuberance ask, "Have you been wearing your tiara the entire day?"

This simple exercise with friends will give you a new perspective on winning the mental game and creating the self-confidence needed for any type of event. Guys, since everyone loves to laugh, your newfound skill of confident humor will also update your first impression status. Even the ladies might give you a second look.

The next step is to improve your "game within the game." They say there is a motive behind every crime. Does that same philosophy hold true for greatness, as in playing at a championship level? See if you can reflect on sports moments when you excelled. What sparked an explosive transformation in a few of the 100 billion neurons in your brain? Was there an emotional story that inspired a great performance? Or was it the logic in a great game plan that maintained your momentum? See if you can pinpoint the source of that game-time motivation. Learning from those experiences and using that knowledge to create awesome sports tags is the key to proper mental preparation. When your mental game of choice has successfully loaded with the right ammo, it will trigger more than random flashes of greatness come game time.

Everyone in sports wants to believe in that "something extra." Chicago Cubs fans depend on Helga the goat to be the game-changer to break the Billy Goat curse from 1945. Decked out in Cubby apparel, Helga changes the entire atmosphere at the local bar. With Helga along to watch the playoffs on the big screen, superstitious fans no longer fear the curse. Unfortunately, this combination of logic and feel-good emotion does not affect game-time performance.

The last time the Cubs won a World Series was in 1908. TVs and radios for the home had not been invented! In 2016, the record 108-year drought finally ended when the Cubs made an astonishing comeback after the Cleveland Indians took a 3-1 lead in the series.

The winner-take-all game 7 proved to be an epic nail-biter as it went into extra innings. During the rain break, the Cubs held a players-only meeting. The focus was on supporting each other and how they had mustered the determination to overcome everything to get to this point. That moment of inspiration would provide the motivation for a dramatic win. The Chicago Cubs once again became World Champions.

This quest to find a greater power is not found in fortune cookies and trinkets or even lucky rituals. *It is found within yourself.* To become the most feared competitor on the field requires expanding your mental game. By combining the athletic powers of your heart and mind, you can expand your arsenal starting with a military weapon or a deck of cards, each loaded with unwavering confidence. Soon, you will be that go-to athlete who can't miss, whose performance is unstoppable, and always "in the zone."

But hold on. We have only begun the journey to find and fill your sports arsenal. God has a game plan that you need to hear. His version of a "something extra" will make a game-changing and possibly life-changing difference. That's the payoff once you learn to unlock God's sports arsenal, you can weaponize every area of your mental game.

# Sports Warehouse

## Chapter 2

The human brain stores a tremendous amount of information and experiences. This inventory of thoughts can be used to excel in everyday life and in sports. Every year the two best teams in pro football end up in the Super Bowl because they have tapped into their most powerful weapon—the mind. Somehow, they have managed to upgrade their mental inventory with sports tags to execute their strengths and take advantage of the opposing team's weaknesses. The experience of playing a near-perfect mental game is now stored some-where between the ears.

In the 2014 Super Bowl, those teams were the Denver Broncos and the Seattle Seahawks. While on the road to acquiring the coveted Super Bowl ring, the Broncos played with mile-high confidence. They looked like invincible warriors—so what happened on Super Bowl Sunday? Why did the Broncos get blown out? They played so poorly even loyal fans were left groaning, "That was a terrible game." "Nothing went right." "Even the first play was a disaster." It took only 12 seconds for the Seahawks to put points on the scoreboard. A botched snap sailed over Quarterback Peyton Manning's head, only to be recovered by him in the end zone for a safety. Just like that it was 0-2, and from that play on, the entire Denver team was thrown out of sync and never recovered in a 43-8 rout.

Such disasters have happened before. The lopsided Seattle-Denver score ranked just fourth on the list of biggest blowouts in Super Bowl history.

What triggered Denver's mental breakdown to achieve 60-game minutes of total embarrassment? Did they forget to pack their Superman t-shirts, accidentally wash all the luck out of their lucky underwear, or did the party atmosphere of Super Bowl week cause a super-sized hangover?

Chances are, it had more to do with their lack of proper mental preparation, than too much party time, or the unpredictable power of luck. Anytime an athlete's heart and mind are pumped-up with fantasies of greatness and lofty dreams of becoming world champions, a quick score by the other team brings it all crashing down. So, to avoid a similar disaster, it's time to explore your mental game, starting with your most powerful weapon—your mind. The assignment is to find the place where upgraded mental tags are weaponized with emotion to trigger greatness. Before you start your venture into the brain's athletic psyche, let's scope out a familiar place where common mental connections are used in everyday life.

First, I want you to take a short journey home without moving from your chair. Simply close your eyes and use your brainpower to visualize your home's TV room. When friends stop by to watch the big game, this is the place to hang out. Suppose those same friends are planning a surprise Super Bowl party at your house. Just in case they pull it off, do a mental count of the seating to see if you need any extra chairs. Got the number? That wasn't so hard, was it?

Take a minute to realize what you have just done. Your stored intellect is not a random pile of memories. Instead, it was created with the ability to departmentalize a wide variety of people, places, and things as well as prized sports moments.

You have the ability to build duplicate copies of your daily surroundings so that you can simplify the tremendous amount of daily information and organize it into a number of virtual rooms. If you are searching for something that you lost, such as a wallet, you can go through each room in the midst of your memory and even zoom in on smaller details. On a larger scale, without this ability, you would never find your car in the parking lot after shopping at Walmart.

Now, see if you can target the place in your consciousness that best resembles a sports related man-cave (or she-shed). This is where your head and heart go to work setting up your "game within the game." All your strategizing takes place by using virtual recordings (videos) of past and present game film and reviewing the game plan. Your prep work is not that hard when all the shelves are filled with great sports moments.

Sadly, this headspace is under-utilized, however, if it is well-stocked and well-organized, your prep time can lead to a big victory on the scoreboard. Since there is enough room to visualize your favorite sports arena, this headspace is best defined as a *"Sports Warehouse."*

The uniqueness of the sports warehouse makes it a valuable tool for other areas of your life. It is designed to create a virtual reality of future get-togethers and store up a perception of how perfect things could be or how you can end up with a total disaster. These upcoming events include first dates, job interviews, a wedding toast to the bride and groom, or a business speech in front of a large group. Any significant event with enough emotion to experience the thrill of victory or the agony of embarrassment would be created at this location.

Since your mental warehouse is engineered to prepare you for any type of upcoming event, time is constantly updating your present inventory of ideas and images. In the case of competitive sports, once the game is over, it's time to bring in the maintenance crew before closing the doors and turning out the lights. By the time you hit the showers, your anticipation of playing a great game or your fear of playing a bad game are now old news. After you enjoy the euphoric high of winning or suffer the pain of losing, those feelings start to diminish. That's because game-day emotions have a limited shelf life before they lose their effectiveness. In order to make room for the next significant event in your life, your old sports inventory is transferred to long-term storage. That extra storeroom in the back of your mind has a sign on the door labeled: "The Glory Days."

## The Prime Directive of Sports

Your mission is to be mentally prepared so you can consistently play your best. This means bringing your sports warehouse back to a game-ready status. When it's filled with all the right weapons, the head and heart feel confident. Without a basic weapon of confidence, it's almost impossible to make a $4^{th}$-quarter comeback or to avoid being blown out.

This leads us to the prime directive in the world of sports. Since your sports warehouse only offers temporary storage, use this rule to avoid inventory control problems:

***Mentally organize what you need to execute!***

In other words, be proactive—be intentional. Set yourself up to win by winning the mental game. That means organizing short-term—long-term goals and anticipating numerous ways to achieve victory. Then, mentally transfer those concepts on paper to the sports psyche. When you can see it happening in your mind, it becomes a self-serving prophecy, and your heart will do everything possible to make your future reality come true.

This directive to come prepared may sound simplistic, but your thoughts *can* set up future experiences, and direct your path toward success. That's why it's important to anticipate what should happen and how to accomplish it—*not* dwell on possible ways to fail.

It's worth mentioning again. The key to succeeding in sports warfare is all about reducing your reaction time. When you're *not* prepared to face adversity, any hesitation or doubt can misdirect your motor neurons and take you out—totally out of the zone. That's why sports tags are your best weapon for gaining an advantage. When you have done the prep work to organize the right skills and combine those skills with a can-do competitive emotion, expect your motor neurons to execute big plays with lightning-fast speed.

Fans cringe when they see a wide-open pro football player drop an easy catch on a critical third downplay. Why did the ball slip through his fingers and drop to the turf? After years of high school and college experience, his mental pathways must be well established, so what caused the brain freeze? Did his heart fear the thought of Kamikaze linebackers zeroing in for an explosive hit, or was his mind so certain the catch would be automatic that he looked down-field too soon? Hard to tell. In either case, his sports inventory was not organized to execute a series of complex mental connections, so his motor neurons were not hitting on all cylinders.

Now do you see the importance of remembering this mantra? A sign saying, "Mentally organize what you need to execute!" should be hanging on the wall of your sports warehouse, or make it into a country song, and print it on all your T-shirts. When this rule to weaponize your game becomes routine, your talent can adapt to become "one better" than the guy you're up against.

Up to this point, the focus has been on the head and heart, but what about the third entity—the soul? What about its need for a spiritual connection?

This concept of using your mental inventory to enhance game-day performance has roots in the book of Luke in the New Testament of the Bible. Some Bible verses are meant for a specific point in time while others describe general principles that can be applied to current areas of your life.

***No good tree bears bad fruit, nor does a bad tree bear good fruit. Each tree is recognized by its own fruit. People do***

> ***not pick figs from thornbushes, or grapes from briers. A good man brings good things out of the good stored up in his heart, and the evil man brings evil things out of the evil stored up in his heart. For the mouth speaks what his heart is full of.***
>
> Luke 6:43-45

If this is your first attempt at deciphering Bible verses, Jesus would frequently make his point by using a lot of imagery and often included a cryptic storyline. In this teaching, Jesus doesn't disappoint. We have a mixed bag of good and bad fruit, good and bad trees, along with good and evil people.

Hopefully, these scriptures didn't sound like everyone needs to plant a fruit tree or the expression, "garbage in—garbage out." Jesus is exposing the power of the heart and the basic operations taking place in its mini-warehouse. The heart is engineered to prepare future words and actions by using your inventory of stored up thoughts. When the mini-warehouse is full, it has a huge effect on your emotional well-being, but if you're not careful, there can be negative consequences. When the mouth is triggered to speak—sometimes it's not for the better.

When someone's words or actions don't line up with the current situation, they have inventory control issues. An example would be a sudden outburst of unjustified anger when celebrating with friends at a nice restaurant. Everyone is left wondering, what has gotten into him?

My friend and pastor, Steve Carter, authored a book called, *The Thing beneath the Thing*. The title is a fairly accurate description of this biblical teaching. Jesus is indicating that one's character is determined by what's going on below the surface.

If you were to visualize the heart as having its own mini-storage unit or if you better relate to a backyard shed, the shelves on one side would hold the “good things” and on the opposite wall are life’s “evil things.” These evil things are capable of hurting others or even yourself. Your mental inventory can weigh you down and depress your emotional well-being, or on the flip side, it can help you become a “good person.” Maybe it’s time to retrain your mindset to hold onto life’s joyful moments and produce some good fruit. How can this be accomplished?

If we were to decode this teaching, it takes a number of variables for a tree to produce “good fruit,” most importantly time and effort. In the same context, the “good things” in life don’t just end up, being stored up by themselves. The results you’re looking for are all about our choices, choices, choices. Dr. Joel Hoomans, a sociologist, claims that we make an average of 35,000 decisions every day.[1] A number that high sounds like the control group is a bunch of pro video gamers, but Dr. Hoomans’s point is clear. During our daily epidemic of busyness, we are faced with an overwhelming number of decisions. So if the wheels of intentionality aren’t turning, you won’t have time to sort out and “store up” the right mental inventory.

You may not realize it, but even a small number of good decisions can create pathways to guide future words and actions. Long ago, King Solomon warned his people how previous thoughts have the power to change your destiny.

***Be careful how you think; your life is shaped by your thoughts.***

Proverbs 4:23 (GNT)

The Bible has been translated into several versions, such as the King James, New International Version, Revised Standard, etc. In some of these versions, the teaching from

Luke 6:43-45 is focused on the heart's limited storage space. These passages use the word "overflow" or "abundance" to picture the heart as an emotional reservoir. Once the heart can't hold any more, it's only a matter of time before the dam breaks and the mouth is forced to speak.

Either translation explains why you don't need a lie detector to read most people. When someone's poker face is not their strong suit, they can't hide a warehouse that's maxed out with doubt, guilt, fear, or especially anger. Just look at the venting process. When the coach or someone else has reached their boiling point, their facial expressions make it obvious what's about to happen. Someone is about to blow up and the other person is about to get an earful of criticism they don't want to hear. The greater the stored-up drama, the louder the emotional explosion.

This spiritual teaching, when applied to sports also validates the directive of mentally organizing what needs to be executed. To consistently develop a pre-game competitive attitude, do you identify with a business-like, get the job done perspective, or seek a more passionate approach? It doesn't matter if you lead with your head or heart, both types of athletes require selecting the "good things" from previous good games and practice sessions. When your sports warehouse is filled with all the right stuff, your game-time superpowers will be unleashed.

If you need to build confidence during the game, the same process takes place. Anytime you flawlessly execute big plays, the positive experience is "stored up" in your sports warehouse. Being surrounded by all of these "accomplishments" will pay big dividends by inspiring the heart, mind, and soul to unite their efforts. They will continue the momentum and create more "good fruit," such as points, goals, and home runs.

Even when game-time disasters happen, you can use the current inventory to restore your intensity by "bringing out the good things." This means drawing on past experiences to recover your momentum before any negative paralysis sets in.

Jesus's teaching on these inventory control issues is one of the most powerful insights in the Bible. It's the cornerstone for other biblical concepts that support a healthy mind space. Since you're developing a sports mindset that weaponizes thoughts with powerful emotions, how can you safely handle the drama without crossing the line and exploding with a regrettable mistake?

Later, we will learn how to deal with explosive inventory control issues and do some warehouse remodeling to utilize the limited space. With clipboard in hand, we will check off the Apostle Paul's "Top 10 list" of "good things" needed to maintain a healthy well-being. Next, we will focus on eliminating all the "evil things" on Matthew's list of undesirables. Also, we will discover the secrets of warehouse maintenance. These house cleansing efforts direct us to "search our hearts" to expose the hidden dirt, and "renew our minds" by taking fearful thoughts "captive," so they can be kicked to the curb.

When you are ready, God is ready with the power and skills to perform an extreme make-over of your mental warehouse. The goal is to be proactive—set yourself up to win. This may require neutralizing a toxic environment caused by last week's loss, so the sooner you ask for God's help, the better. Once you have finished with God's restoration plan, there will be enough space for the heart, mind, and soul to feel confident and ready to handle any situation. It's a whole new world when you're connected to the freedom and "peace of God, which transcends all understanding." (Philippians 4:7)

In contrast to the symbolism Jesus used to make his point, the Apostle Paul was more direct on a number of subjects, including the practicality of mental preparation.

## Chapter 2

> ***Do you not know that in a race all the runners run, but only one receives the prize? So run that you may obtain it. Every athlete exercises self-control in all things. They do it to receive a perishable wreath, but we an imperishable. So I do not run aimlessly; I do not box as one beating the air. But I discipline my body and keep it under control, lest after preaching to others I myself should be disqualified.***
>
> 1 Corinthians 9:24-27 (ESV)

When Paul wrote this in his letter to the church in Corinth, he was clearly living by the sport's rule to "Target what matters most." Like an athlete who is all about disciplining his body and not showing off with shadow boxing fantasies or running aimlessly, Paul was not going to let poor mental preparation result in poor preaching, which would discredit him from receiving God's heavenly reward.

In sports, keeping one's eye on the prize is not about luck; it is about using self-control. As Paul noted over 2000 years ago, "Every athlete exercises self-control in all things." Maintaining a disciplined attitude is huge—a critical weapon for developing greatness. Even today, you could call it the wild card in completing any successful mission. Regrettably, with all the celebrity status surrounding the game, most athletes aren't willing to sacrifice the extra mental or physical prep time needed to stand above the competition. What distractions are keeping you from focusing on what's important?

### Heart Psychology 101

Most people see the human heart as the source of Valentine's Day emotions. To them, it generates feelings of love, affection, and friendship—not recognized as a temporary storage unit as Jesus described in Luke 6:45 and Matthew 12:34-35. Other biblical accounts describe the heart as an individual entity. The Apostle Peter acknowledged your "hidden person of the heart" in 1 Peter 3:4 ESV and the Apostle Paul encouraged people to open the eyes of their hearts in Ephesians 1:18. These descriptions of the heart all define your subconscious psyche, the deep center of one's existence. That is until a verse on the "soul" pops up with the same definition. To further complicate things, the head and the heart normally have separate identities until a verse pops up where they share the same attributes. Don't worry. Usually, you can decipher the implied psychology of the "heart" based on the context of how it is used.

Humans are complicated, so it's easy to see why they often need help with their physical and psychological well-being. It's as if three separate entities (people) are crowded together in your consciousness. When the current state of mind is determined by the conflict and/or compromise taking place within the heart, mind, and soul, even little issues can be blown out of proportion. That's why help is on the way. Jesus made this promise to send a fourth entity, the Holy Spirit—to mediate your jam-packed psyche: "for if I don't go away, the Counselor won't come to you." (John 16:7 WEB)

Since you're dealing with the head and the heart as individual entities, let's simplify the mental game. See if you can picture the sports warehouse as the building where they report for active duty. They are proficient in attaching descriptive sports tags and filling the shelves with weaponized thoughts. It's a job they love doing, but since anyone can be a critic, there is a natural tendency to dwell on the negatives or be misled by faulty expectations.

The secret to greatness, however, is to contribute something productive instead of being a critic. Choose the type of inventory that can make a positive impact. The stored-up stories and strategies should be "good things" that excite your heart and make your head feel smart. Without their stamp of approval on all of the sports related content, it's tough to stay in the zone.

You could keep it simple and say the mental game only happens inside the sports warehouse, but why not expand your military mindset? If you're going to create a virtual reality, why not create an entire "military base of operations."

Think of your potential when the head and heart are fully trained to work at the "Armory." They can build performance-enhanced weapons with the firepower to drastically increase the trajectory of your talent. Can you picture yourself with a renewed attitude of invincibility? You can achieve this!

The military base of operations is God's gift to everyone, not just athletes. God's handiwork is always exceptional, and your base of operations comes complete with everything you need for any type of warfare. Besides having an impregnable armory to build an arsenal of weapons and a huge sports warehouse to store game information, there is a central headquarters to coordinate every mission. Because of the military importance of the command center, you are instructed to provide the extra protection needed to "guard" God's classified orders and keep them from falling into enemy hands.

> ***My son, keep my words and store up my commands within you ... guard my teachings as the apple of your eye ... write them on the tablet of your heart.***
>
> Proverbs 7:1-3

When King Solomon wrote these verses 3,000 years ago, he probably didn't realize how timeless God's words would be. They indicate that an electronic tablet is standard equipment located inside the "Strategic Command Center."

Your tablet is not only synced to maintain your sports warehouse and weapons armory but can run factory-installed applications. One of the best apps converts the entire base of operations from "stand-by mode" into "combat mode." This program will not only launch a dangerous competitive attitude but activate your built-in radar system. Now you can target and if necessary, track your adversary by using the eyes in the back of your head. That inside information helps you gain an advantage by anticipating your opponent's next move.

When it comes to maintaining a "combat mode" mindset, I'm convinced that athletes blow it more often in this area of the game than in any other. Momentum is not static, so a big play changes the flow of the game, and big plays require big mental breakdowns by the other team. Next time you are watching your favorite sporting event, take note of how many times the momentum changes when athletes miss the mark. In almost every sport the mental failures to target and track the ball are plentiful. Most athletes are clueless about this military app or how it can keep your built-in radar switched on for the entire game. Later, we will take a detailed look at how this sports tag can track, target, and even calculate the ball's point of impact. It will help you maintain your laser focus and eliminate the coach's stern reminder to "Get your head in the game!"

The military base of operations, complete with its sports warfare package, is a part of God's blessing to you. It works with the grand plan God had in mind when he created Adam and Eve. We find the birth of the military base and its unique mission statement in the first book of the Bible.

> ***God blessed them and said to them, "Be fruitful and increase in number, fill the earth and subdue it.***

## Chapter 2

***Rule over the fish in the sea and the birds in the sky and over every living creature that moves on the ground."***

Genesis 1:28

God's plan started with creating a beautiful planet to support humans and filling it with unbelievable wildlife. Most people have no trouble understanding God's reasoning behind preserving the human race by populating the planet, but when it comes to ruling over all the animals, some don't get the big picture. You are a hunter with a hunter's heart, and God has given you a fearless level of confidence to enter an untamed world. It's a big deal that God's first blessing to mankind included a sophisticated set of skills to use when in "hunting mode." These hunting skills are not only useful for recognizing and dealing with danger in the wild, but can transcend into other areas, such as protecting God's kingdom in times of spiritual warfare, even during a sporting event.

Originally, God designed these hunting skills as weapons for our survival on a planet filled with wild animals. The tagging and radar tracking equipment were necessary not only to protect the family but to pursue and subdue every flying, walking, or swimming creature that would fit on the barbecue grill.

At some point, grocery stores added a meat department, so the need to hunt for wild game morphed into a limited sport. But the desire God placed in the hunter's heart remained. The thrill of capturing your prey and celebrating the successful hunt with a feast slowly transitioned into competitive sporting events and tailgate parties. Now you know why there is something special, almost spiritual about sharing burnt brats on the grill with fellow sports enthusiasts. It's because this first biblical blessing was hard-wired into your DNA, and even today inspires tailgate parties all around the world.

# Military Base of Operations

## Chapter 3

One of the most talked-about emotions in sports is confidence. The military base is where a warrior's heart takes it to the next level. This is where battle-ready emotions are generated, tagged to sports situations, and stored to be used as powerful game-time motivators. That is why your stored level of self-assurance has a big effect on who you are and what you do. If you do not control your inventory of emotions and silence your fears, negativity will take over ... slam the vault door on the sports warehouse and scramble the access code to lock out your talent.

The mental exercise at the end of chapter 1 involved loading self-confidence for a social event. It was probably your first planned mission calling for logistical support when gathering with friends. Your head and heart were assigned to organize your mental inventory. By utilizing a modified version of the first impression process, you upgraded your visual images of friends and relatives with humorous tags that allowed you to set the tone. We described this progression as preparing a weapon or card of verbal confidence. When you're into sports, it is important to use this same process. Like LeBron, you can combine fundamental skills with a competitive passion for an impressive performance.

Although, building a .50 caliber military-grade weapon of confidence for your weapons armory will pique your interest, it is equally important to spend prep time revamping the sports warehouse. Storing up a "good sports" inventory produces great sports moments, but what about dealing with past failures—the gut-wrenching disasters that should be thrown out? Unintentionally hanging on to "bad fruit" can stink up your destiny. Let's not forget that the head and heart personally tag every significant event and place it in the sports warehouse. Though you do not intend to end up with so many "bad things," all game situations are tagged as either "good" or "bad" depending on the outcome.

When the game ends, the mistakes you've made are like reruns of an old TV show, and normally packed up for long-term storage. The only reason the "dreadful things" hang around is because your heart will not permit them to leave, not without resolving the conflict or guilt. It makes no sense to play the blame game to deny your responsibility in the matter, so *stop*! Do not let the past irritate you. Soothe your heart-felt wounds by changing the negative tags and send them packing before they become emotional scars.

It has been said, "You only get one chance to make a first impression." That is because mental tags are extremely hard to change. In a game situation, there are no do-overs or even a delete key that lets you remove a previous game mistake from your memory. Depressing sports experiences can, however, be modified, but it takes more than faking a positive attitude to rewrite a bad sports tag.

## Disarming Weaponized Drama

Before tackling some of your haunting sports disasters, put the power of your competitive psyche to work revamping your Top-10 List of "What I hate doing at practice." Hate is a powerful emotion that can be weaponized to motivate hearts and minds, but the results are unpredictable. How can hate-filled experiences be disarmed? Fortunately, your miserable attitude towards practice drills does not have the same holding power as regrettable game-changing mistakes, so these tags are relatively easy to deal with. Pick out a practice drill near the top of your list and see if you can disarm the negative feelings and re-tag the situation into something more productive.

Let's say your favorite drill to hate is wind sprints. As boring as they may be, sports is about speed. If you want to be fast, you have to think fast. Instead of dragging yourself through this drill, add a mental image that would make you feel the "need for speed." Imagine, opening the doors to your sports warehouse and seeing a combat fighter or muscle car or a 225-hp jet ski (for swimmers). The perceived experience of sitting in the seat and revving up the engine will inspire the power and speed they represent. Now, when it's time for wind sprints, think of this new image and listen to the scream of a jet engine or the deep rumble of unlimited horsepower. This can be a *pain changer*.

The process of repurposing a previous hate-filled tag is simple. When a new storyline contains more emotional horsepower than the previous one, it can disarm the negativity. The thought of wind sprints will no longer be weaponized to inflict excruciating pain. Instead, you will enjoy revving up your engine before the coach blows the whistle.

After mastering this re-tagging process on hated practice drills, tackle team chemistry. Competitiveness can bring regrettable words that do inexcusable damage, so try improving one of your rocky relationships. Hopefully, you can start the forgiveness process by going to that person and admitting that it was your fault. If that is not the case, then picture the teammate's face in your mind and see if you can start the healing process by finding some "good things" about that person. Changing your emotional focus will eventually upgrade your mental tags and limit the social weirdness that comes from unsettled grievances or angry thoughts of retaliation. That teammate may still irritate you to no end, but during games, you can overcome the distraction when teamwork is needed to secure the win.

The final step in this sports warehouse clean-up process is to deal with your haunting mistakes—the ones witnessed by all the fans and let your teammates down. These images of failure are tougher to deal with because they have been weaponized with extra guilt or embarrassment. Emotion can multiply their size and weight by one hundred times. Negative emotion has the lingering power to block your talent by having you second-guess your ability. These confidence blockers will make you hesitate when a gold medal or championship trophy is within reach.

Disarming any defeatist emotional drama or repairing relationships is no quick fix. It's not as if you can cut and paste negative images and emotions. But you can perform an upgrade on these bad memories. In sports, this can be done by rewriting the emotional tags and connecting with better fundamental skills. Combining the right skillset with newfound confidence, or better yet, aggressiveness, can transform a sports experience from crippling to achievable and make it game-ready. Then, when it comes time to execute a similar play, there won't be any negative paralysis to stop you from doing it the right way.

Most of the inventory in your mental warehouse is remarkably diverse, so do not limit this clean-up process to just sports tags. You do have a life, and the negative tags associated with your real-life circumstances can take you on an emotional roller coaster. To help us slow down that heart-pounding ride and live a life filled with joy, confidence, and contentment, the Apostle Paul shows us how to hit the brakes. The following list of real-life tags will make sure God's stamp of approval is on all the "good things." When your mental warehouse is filled with high-quality thoughts, you can experience the "best day ever."

***Finally, brothers and sisters,***
***whatever is true, whatever is noble,***
***whatever is right, whatever is pure,***
***whatever is lovely, whatever is***

***admirable—if anything is excellent or praiseworthy—think about such things.***

Philippians 4:8

This directive from the Apostle Paul resonates with Jesus' teaching to have the right inventory on the shelves of your mental warehouse. If you were to combine these two concepts, Jesus is giving you the logistics for warehouse management and the Apostle Paul is labeling the shelves.

If you're serious about winning in the game of everyday life, then look up the definition of each of Paul's labels and see how they can improve current situations. Some of these biblical tags cater to the mind's sense of logic, while others are for the heart to embrace, and if anything is "excellent or praiseworthy," then it meets the needs of both mindsets. Use this knowledge to mentally review your current inventory and restock any shelves that might be low on "good things." This type of intentionality will re-focus your thought process to grab more "good things" as they rush through your day.

In some African villages, the danger of being eaten by a lion is always present. The fearful tag attached to that possible situation is so powerful that children will have night terrors of being chased by a lion. In this situation, it takes a new storyline, one with the strength and courage to disarm the heart-racing tag. Parents will tell their children to fight back in their dreams—to stop running, stand up to the lion, and scream as loud as they can until it runs away.

A simplified version for improving your mental and emotional wellness would be to count your blessings every day. By taking control of your thought process, you will be developing an "attitude of gratitude" which results in a major swing towards positivity.

What about the sports tags that have an emotional bond that is just too strong to break, and even an ear-piercing scream won't help? In those situations, the help of a higher power will be required, and God specializes in disarming weaponized tags. In chapter 8, we will focus on neutralizing the traumatizing effect of performance anxiety and the art of "letting go."

Getting back to your military base of operations. One of the highlights of the Strategic Command Center is the home theater system. Seeing images in your mind is commonly referred to as using your mind's eye or using the theater of your mind. Regardless of how you label it, this part of the brain can replay your favorite blockbuster movie scenes and create a virtual reality of all types of sports scenarios. The big screen in the Strategic Command Center can also be used to check out the current inventory of weapons in the armory and to upgrade the sports tags in the sports warehouse.

Anytime you visualize something on the big screen, it ends up in the sports warehouse. Imagining ways to use your best weapons will make sure they are locked and loaded, ready for your next battle. Visualizing your game plan also gives you a military advantage. It establishes mental pathways that reduce reaction time, which gives you a step-up on your opponent. It's another benefit of following the prime directive: "Mentally organizing what you need to execute."

LeBron James once described how he started using his mental abilities in high school basketball. He realized he had a knack for remembering past tendencies from opposing teams' offensive and defensive sets. Replicating those previous situations in the theater of his mind let him mentally organize his sports inventory. LeBron even remembered how certain players defend his various scoring drives. By mentally rehearsing these game situations, he was able to anticipate the weaknesses of certain defenders. This type of positive visualization helped steer him to the right place at the right time on the basketball court. LeBron's tactics to gain an advantage helped both the Miami Heat and the Cleveland

Cavaliers win world championships.

LeBron is in good company when it comes to organizing his military base of operations. Let's look at other professional athletes who have jam-packed their sports warehouse with game-winning images.

Jerry Rice consistently excelled on the football field. His ability to develop a reliable mental game earned him numerous NFL records that may never be broken. While the average active life in the NFL is 3 years, Jerry's career lasted 20. Drafted by the San Francisco 49ers, Jerry spent his first 15 years as their go-to wide receiver. Jerry is generally regarded as the greatest wide receiver in NFL history. With his work ethic and consistency, Rice created the blueprint for all wide receivers to follow.

In his book, *Jerry Rice Go Long!*, he talked about how he got a little nervous before games. Even with all his achievements, Jerry suffered from pre-game performance anxiety, which sometimes caused sleepless nights before games. To calm down he would run his pass-routes over and over in his mind, playing out different scenarios to combat the fear of letting his team down.

Jerry did not realize that his technique of fighting back the pre-game jitters was his way of weaponizing his sports warehouse with the right emotional inventory. This strategy of visualizing numerous first-down catches and end-zone scoring opportunities helped him replace performance anxiety with performance confidence.

Another one of Jerry's secrets was keeping his mental inventory of scoring plays as close to reality as possible. "Keep it real" is another important sports rule of engagement. Mentally, there is an enormous difference between saying you're going to do something and replicating 10 realistic scoring opportunities in your mind's virtual reality. If you want actual game-time experiences to come true, it's critical to keep your perception of future events as close to reality as possible. But beware, when the number of choreographed touchdown dances exceeds the number of realistic scoring plays, your mental inventory has been corrupted by violating the "keep it real" rule.

Joe Montana, a Hall of Fame quarterback, earned three Super Bowl rings with the 49ers with the help of Jerry Rice's receiving skills. During games, Joe would walk up to the line of scrimmage with a distant look or blank stare on his face. What was he doing? Commentators would say that he was checking off his receivers. This was true, but was there more to the story? Could Joe have been detailing the offensive play at his Strategic Command Center, preparing a big picture of the scoring opportunities before the play started? His ability to mentally organize his entire base of operations for this future play allowed him to execute the right decisions at the right time. This earned Joe the reputation of being as "cool as the underside of a pillow," even in the heated final seconds of a game-winning drive.

Tiger Woods is among the most successful golfers of all time and was one of the highest-paid athletes in the world for several years. Woods has broken numerous golf records. He has been ranked number one in the world for the most consecutive weeks and holds the record of leading the *Forbes* money list for 10 different seasons. He is the youngest player to achieve the career Grand Slam and win 50 PGA tournaments.

When Tiger Woods steps onto the tee box for his opening drive, he does more than just tee up his lucky ball and swing. Tiger likes to visualize every shot as being perfect. During his practice swing, he imagines the arc of the ball and where it will land before it bounces on the green and rolls toward the flag. This visual imagery has informed Strategic Command of essential mental connections. It allows him to measure the distance to the pin, the force to drive the club, the wind speed and direction, along with the condition of the green *before he launches the ball.*

In Olympic downhill racing, the outcome is measured in fractions of a second. The top skiers spend a great deal of time mentally preparing for each run down the course. They visualize the proper entry into each turn on the slope in hopes of maintaining maximum speed. A few hundredths of a second can make all the difference between bringing home the gold medal or going home empty-handed.

## Light Bulb Moment!

By now you should have a good idea of how great athletes deal with mental preparation. Behind the vault door protecting the military base of operations, we find the secret to a successful athlete's mental game—a sports warehouse. Most likely filled with images of a basketball court, a football field, a golf course, or a snow-covered mountain slope.

Top athletes like Joe Montana and Tiger Woods have found a way to utilize their command center and sports warehouse to create clear 360-degree mental images. These future events contain all the competitive factors yet limit all the chaos that comes with competing. Otherwise, the head and heart would be distracted by all the rambunctious fan noise, eye-catching cheerleaders, and ever-present media. When these athletes can visualize the big picture, they are ready to execute big plays. Sports commentators will say, "He read it perfectly," or "He must have eyes in the back of his head." This is what happens when you have anticipated these game situations in your command center. Your internal perspective is like that *Star Wars* scene where officers are gathered around a table viewing holographic images of an intergalactic battle zone.

# Chapter 3

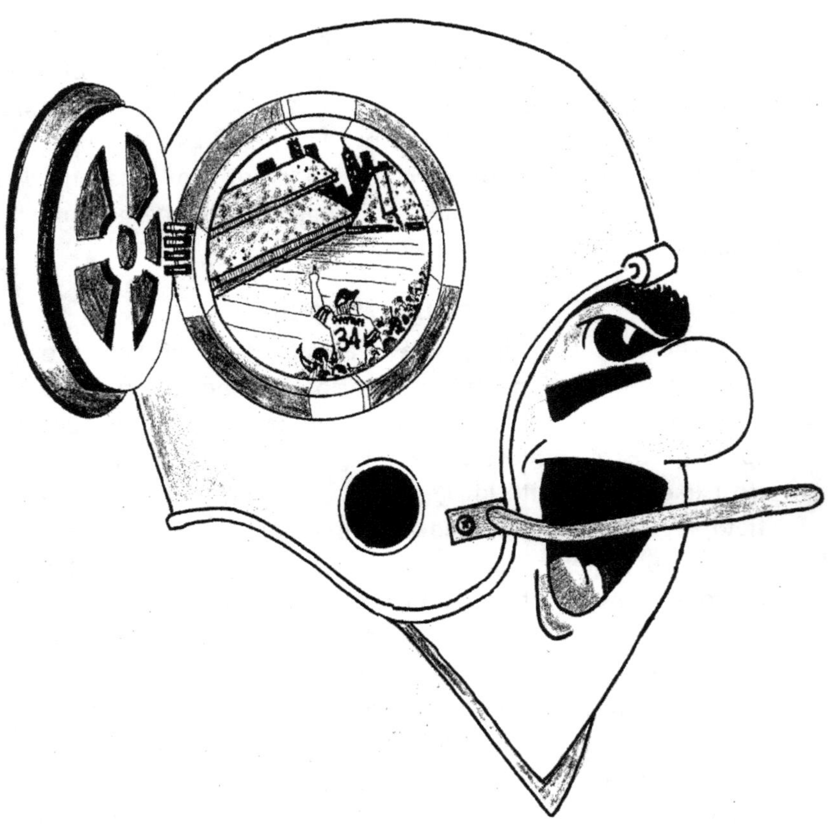


When the Strategic Command Center is fully operational, quarterbacks will frequently use this vantage point to target an open receiver. Without X-ray vision to see through the linemen, they take a visible piece of their field of view and put together a 3-D picture needed for a touchdown opportunity.

## *TURBO-BOOST*

During a game, when excitement and emotion are running high, the Strategic Command Center is revved-up to process everything at a much higher speed. Operating at game speed changes the relationship between the command center and the sports warehouse. The command center is now totally dependent on the contents inside the sports warehouse. If you have not spent the time to mentally organize what needs to be executed, your performance can be as pitiful as that of a drunk driver pulled over by the police. Even the simple task of falling on a loose football can become impossible, and your disastrous play will be forever immortalized on a sports blooper video.

While coaching knee-high soccer players, I used a simple story to explain how the brain runs at two different speeds. I would start by asking, "Who has ridden in the car when Grandma is driving?" Almost all the kids raised their hands. Then I would ask if they noticed that Grandma takes a long time to react to a green light and hit the gas. Since most had no clue what I was saying, I would then ask whether Grandma moves quickly or slowly around the house. Most said "slowly." Then I would say, "When you are at Grandma's house, what would happen if you blew up a paper bag, snuck up behind her, and popped the bag?" They would smile and laugh after picturing the outcome of the situation.

Why I asked, would Grandma who moved so slowly, suddenly be so fast? I explained it was because her brain works at two different speeds. Normal processing speed is used most of the time, and high-speed kicks in when she gets overwhelmed with emotion. In her case, the loud noise created fear.

Back when I was coaching kids, *Knight Rider* was a popular TV show. It featured a talking car, a big hit with young boys. One of the car's gadgets was a turbo-boost button that engaged instant acceleration. The conclusion for the mini soccer players was: "When you are on the soccer field, I want you to push that turbo-boost button so your brain is running at high speed. Then you can react quicker than Grandma and run faster than anyone on the soccer field."

The turbo-boost image provided the players with a sports tag they could visualize, and that red button never left the command center. A sports tag doesn't need to be tagged to a person or a specific sports situation. Internal coaching instructions can be connected to any object so long as you use the right emotion to make it work.

The thought of driving a tricked-out car provided the storyline needed for these young soccer players to transform their performance. In this case, it was easy for these young athletes to just push the button and speed up their mental game. This simple sports tag did what it was supposed to do: It enhanced their decision-making abilities as well as improved their physical game.

Muhammad Ali's famous line "I float like a butterfly, then sting like a bee" is a good analogy of how *The Champ* effortlessly disposed of his opponents by mentally changing speed. His style of gracefully floating around the ring enabled him to out-dance his opponent without using the mental quickness needed for landing a punch. Patiently, Ali waited for the right opportunity to switch to high speed. Then he would fire off a powerful round of punches that dazed his opponent or delivered the knockout blow.

Just how fast is fast when every area of the military base is triggered to run at game speed? Some researchers claim that the human mind can pick up images at $1/24^{th}$ of a second. Yet, the average person normally has a one-second reaction time. Advertisers on TV will not flash pictures of their products any faster than that, or most people won't get it. In sports, if it takes an athlete one second to figure out where the ball is going, it's too late to react.

One of the unique qualities of the Strategic Command Center is the ability to process visual information. After the win, quarterbacks and receivers often comment about the benefit of having a sports perspective. They describe how the game-breaking play seemed to unfold in slow motion, as if watching an instant replay. When the processing power in the command center is switched to high speed, the images being processed are slowed down, giving athletes time to react and make the big play.

The specialized actions going on inside the military base are endless. Thus, two athletes who play the same position on the same team will have different inventories of mental pictures and sports tags. This is because of the way they approach the mental game. Each athlete has to satisfy a hungry head and heart with the type of tags they crave. The best way to maintain a well-stocked mental inventory is to look at the appetites of pro athletes.

Before game time, do you need your sports warehouse filled to capacity to feel confident? Jerry Rice loaded his mental warehouse with images of scoring opportunities. When he reviewed notable game film, he likely memorized an opponent's behaviors and tagged them with the appropriate counter-measures.

During a game, do you need to see the big picture before the play starts? You may need to envision how the entire play will be organized. That would be similar to the process Joe Montana and Tiger Woods use. Whether preparing a single play to use during the game or a pre-game collection of scoring situations, once your command center is ready to execute the right strategy, you can feel confident in your abilities.

Maybe your priority is to focus on the emotional part of the game instead of studying the other team. Many athletes are reminded of their potential talent by connecting an emotional storyline to a real object. Pro football athletes have been caught wearing Superman T-shirts in the weight room, inspiring their internal "man of steel." After sacking a quarterback, a defensive player will cast an imaginary fishing pole to symbolize the feeling of reeling in the big one. Some receivers, usually wearing a Jets uniform, will spread their arms and imitate a military fighter jet celebrating a fly-by over the end zone after scoring a touchdown. Parking a fighter jet in the sports warehouse could also provide the motivation for extra speed and maneuverability to fly through the defense.

Are we on the verge of making a T-shirt or fishing pole a "lucky" charm? As you can surmise, an athlete seeking an intellectual rationale would not give any credibility to such silliness. Neither the object nor the accompanying performance is very professional. Yet, athletes seeking to weaponize their heart-inspired moment would argue that it organizes fundamental skills and generates enough emotion to become a catalyst for explosive greatness. The arguments from both are justified; however, if you do add an object to improve the emotional part of your mental game, keep it simple. Be creative and have fun, just make sure it doesn't get you or your teammates in trouble.

The grand scheme is to unlock the potential of the military base by coordinating your command center with the sports warehouse and armory. The majority of pro athletes we have examined are focused on using a logical approach to establish a tone of confidence in every area of their game. Even the images that seem entertaining are based on common sense. The methodology these athletes are using to fill the sports warehouse falls under the guidelines of the top-three rules of sports warfare:

(1) "Mentally organize what you need to execute!"
(2) "Target what matters most."
(3) "Keep it real."

When looking at the distinctions between playing with heart or strategizing with the mind, we covered athletes who have chosen to satisfy the needs of the mind *first*. By spending time analyzing the game plan, the heart will see the big picture and underwrite an emotional storyline as part of the sports tag. When such prep work creates a high level of unstoppable confidence, it's like fueling up with high octane rocket fuel. The entire military base is about to ignite an explosive transformation in athletic performance.

A Typical Sports Transformation

## Chapter 3

When your military base of operation is prepared to face any type of adversity, game-day distractions now seem small and insignificant. Any attempt to diminish the confidence level between your ears will fail. Even 80,000 hostile fans howling on a third-down conversion can't shake your determination.

Now you know why so many NFL teams script the first 15 plays of the game. This mental exercise transforms the entire team's intensity from stand-by to combat mode. The game plan also unifies team confidence by assessing threats and offering ways to gain an advantage. Now that you know your enemy's vulnerabilities, it is time to roll out the initial strike-package lined up in the sports warehouse. But remember, the physical pre-game warm-ups are also an important part of mental preparation. Use that time to tune-up your motor neurons by making game-speed connections.

When the benefits from your prep work destroy the internal chaos, your military base will be at full-alert, ready to trigger phenomenal game moments. As your intensity grows, the payoff will come with big dividends, even if that bonus is only an extra step on your opponent. That extra step could be the game-changer!

# Sports Armory Weapons of Emotion

## Chapter 4

From biblical warriors to today's professional athletes, many have sought to prepare themselves mentally before going into battle. The desire to know your opponents and learn their weaknesses is not a new idea. Such warriors have been searching for ways to ensure victory for centuries.

As we have learned, gaining a military advantage will inspire the head and heart to fight and conquer. When you strategize, you weaponize the thoughts in your head, but what about the heart? If you still don't understand the heart's motivation ... even a simple story can bring powerful emotions to life. If you can reach this level of emotion it triggers an attitude adjustment. To better weaponize the emotional part of your game to improve performance, consider the deathmatch between David and Goliath in the Old Testament of the Bible.

Goliath was a mountain of a man, standing over 9 feet tall. During Shaquille O'Neal's reign of dominance as an NBA center, fans thought of him as an overpowering giant as well. But weighing in at 325 pounds and towering at 7'1", Shaq was a teddy bear next to Goliath. Everything about the oversized Goliath was unstoppable; even his mouth ran non-stop for 40 days with name-calling and insults. Goliath would definitely be a crowd-pleaser for today's fans who love trash-talking superstars.

The epic biblical battle between the Israelites and the Philistines started with a show of manpower and muscle as thousands of soldiers lined up on each side of the ravine. The Israelite army faced the much-feared Goliath and his Philistine army. Each day for the next 40 days, Goliath stepped forward to take center stage. Boastfully he strutted along the line of soldiers challenging someone from the Israelite army (anyone whose armor was not shaking from fear) to step forward and fight him. Whoever survived this man-to-man conflict would win the battle and force the other army to surrender. The Bible notes Goliath's daily outpouring of trash-talk:

> ***As he [David] was talking with them, Goliath, the Philistine champion from Gath, stepped out from his lines and shouted his usual defiance, and David heard it. Whenever the Israelites saw the man, they all fled from him in great fear.***
>
> 1 Samuel 17:23-24

The days went by, and no one would step forward to accept Goliath's challenge. In fact, the fearless Goliath had a bark as big as his body; his intimidating threats rattled the confidence of the Israelite soldiers to the point where "they all ran from him in great fear."

The lone exception was a young shepherd boy named David, who was 17 at most and considered a scrawny teenager at best. The trash-talk echoed in David's head until he mustered up the courage to accept Goliath's challenge and enter the battlefield carrying only a staff and a sling. Goliath, on the other hand, was armed with a sword almost as tall as David and enough tactical body armor to build a small tank. Anyone could see that David was extremely outgunned and out-muscled and must have a death wish. Once Goliath realized that the approaching soldier was only a boy, his big mouth started to bellow.

***He said to David, "Am I a dog, that you come at me with sticks?" And the Philistine cursed David by his gods.***

1 Samuel 17:43

Goliath was insulted that David was not the elite Israelite warrior he expected. This was his way of saying, "Is that all you got? The best you can come up with is a big stick. A dog's toy is your weapon to fight against me? Take your best shot, kid!" He hurled more insults before he spoke his last defiant words to intimidate David.

***"Come here," he said, "and I'll give your flesh to the birds and the wild animals!"***

1 Samuel 17:44

In today's language, the same taunting quote would be, "I'm going to feed your butt to the buzzards!"

David didn't back down from the loud-mouthed giant and held his own by giving Goliath the real game plan.

***"This day the LORD will deliver you into my hands, and I'll strike you down and cut off your head. This very day I will give the carcasses of the Philistine army to the birds and the wild animals, and the whole world will know that there is a God in Israel."***

With a stone in his sling, David started his windup. Once the stone gained maximum speed, he released it ... and *bam!* With incredible accuracy the stone hit Goliath right between the eyes. He toppled over like a huge redwood tree in the forest, hitting the ground with a thud. David ran over to Goliath, borrowed his super-sized sword, and whacked off Goliath's head. He held it up by the hair, and the crowd went ***WILD!*** With the Philistine champion dead, the Israelites' greatest fear had just been eliminated. By all the cheering, you would've thought they just won the Super Bowl!

On the Philistine side, it was another story. Their superstar was done, toast, and dead. Since they depended on Goliath to be their indestructible leader, there was disbelief and a stone-cold silence along the entire battle line.

Looking at the context of this story, many of the soldiers on both sides were probably farmers, between planting and harvesting seasons. Thousands of full-time die-hard soldiers would not have debated for 40 days about who goes first. On the Israelite side, fear dominated their thoughts and conversation. On the Philistine side, camp life had been a different story. They were there to support Goliath and were expecting him to do all the fighting. Their ultimate challenge was to become the best heckler behind their trash-talking superhero. Every day was showtime as they lined up behind the theatrics of their invincible giant.

When David raised high the severed head of Goliath, their taunting chants fell silent and their arrogant confidence gave way to fear. Their "Kill them all!" attitude became "Run for your lives!" as the adrenalin-filled Israelites charged. As the Philistines bolted from the battlefield, their war plans for an easy victory ended with a blood-spattered trail of dead bodies.

Why would God want a gruesome and bloody story like this in the Bible? The big, unbeatable, loud-mouthed giant gets taken down by an inexperienced *teenager*! From a pro athlete's perspective, could it be a warning about the *Sports Illustrated* jinx? When they make the magazine's front page and strut around with a big head, they can expect to be knocked down to size the following week. Perhaps NFL superstars should also take notice; You must show up with more than a reputation. Overconfidence can end the Super Bowl dreams of a highly favored team at the hand of a younger and less experienced team. (Google "Super Bowl I.")

On another level, is this story about David being driven by a heartfelt passion? Let's face it. The odds of failure were overwhelming. David was too young and inexperienced and lacked the credentials to be an elite warrior. His analytical mind had to be screaming, "RETREAT, RETREAT!" before the battle started, but none of that would rattle his courage. **Why?** His warrior heart was in control.

Maybe God will present you with opportunities to do great things, but giants stand in the way. Will you be able to step up and lead with a passionate heart and not be paralyzed by impossible odds spewing out of an intellectual mind?

The negative paralysis you're feeling did not come from God or his plan, but from *you*. After doing the prep work to feel confident, you threw away that confidence by creating game-time doubts. God is on your side and wants you to stand tall and face your giants. Like David, you may *not* have all the qualifications, but there is no need to be timid like the Israelite soldiers who "all fled from him (Goliath) in great fear." Just remember what 2 Timothy 1:7 says: "For the spirit God gave us does not make us timid, but gives us power..."

God knows about your search for that "something extra" to build confidence and he uses David's great battle to add heart-pounding weapons to your arsenal. These powerful weapons of emotion help you prepare for the quest that God has planned for you. When you are shaking your head at impossible odds, God plans to send you into battle armed with a warrior's relentless courage. What is courage?

> ***"Courage is being scared to death... and saddling up anyway."***
>
> John Wayne

The trials you face are designed to toughen your warrior heart with power and determination. That means weaponizing the same emotions David used to battle his giant. Being prepared for unexpected situations will require more than one weapon in your arsenal. To discover the best weapons to increase your firepower, let's turn to the prequel of David's historic battle.

## Invincible Warriors Wanted!

Wishing to attract only the best and most confident warriors, King Saul offered a "Kill Goliath" compensation package. Who could refuse such an offer—a chance to show off one's combat skills and then be rewarded with a goatskin sack full of money? Since gold was the currency of choice in that day, we are talking about a sizable pot of gold, along with tax-exempt status. But that's not all: The package deal also included the king's beautiful daughter. This was a chance to marry up without any worry of rejection.

A pot of tax-free gold and a gorgeous princess's hand in marriage should have sealed the deal and have the top warriors in Israel attacking each other for a chance to fight the Philistine. The only problem was that the Philistine in question was the giant Goliath, and the challenge was surviving the battle with enough functional body parts intact to enjoy the rewards.

## David Gets the Green Light

A week or so before the historic battle, only young David was brave (or some would say foolish) enough to entertain King Saul's help-wanted ad. Before David could start his journey to fame and the red-carpet treatment, he had to secure the king's endorsement. Making a good first impression is everything, especially when trying to prove you are the man for the job. David's appearance left King Saul unconvinced.

***Saul said, "You are not able to go out against this Philistine and fight him; you are only a young man, and he has been a warrior from his youth."***

1 Samuel 17:33

Saul was trying to give David the big, big picture of his worthy opponent. He pointed to the fact that David was still considered a boy and had not heard of Goliath's extensive training as a skilled warrior or the fact that he was the Philistine champion of Gath. This title meant Goliath was undefeated, even from an early age.

Around the Philistine campfires, tales of Goliath's youthful conquests were even taller than the man himself. As the embellished story goes, Goliath was such a huge baby, he was born standing up. The first words out of his big mouth were grumblings about why the delivery took so long. Before his first birthday party, his parents stared in wide-eyed astonishment as baby Goliath picked up his mom's favorite dagger to make his first kill on a small four-legged creature. The lizard would later serve as a crunchy snack before Goliath marched off to adolescent warrior's boot camp. With his bulging baby muscles, he earned the rookie warrior award before finishing preschool.

Chapter 4

**Defiant Baby-G**
**Ready for Sword Training Class**

In King Saul's mind, David was no match for Goliath. Young David lacked the talent, skill, and confidence that come from formal training and battle experience. King Saul felt David was guilty of having a pretentious confidence, a common trait found among many of today's top pro athletes. When not playing their best, they borrow a contagious confidence from other teammates who are dominating a game. This borrowed energy can ignite an all-star performance, but it is a phony confidence that flames-out after losing a big lead.

How did David truly conquer his fears? Where did his undeniable courage come from? What would motivate the heart of a shepherd boy to step up and fight the giant ahead of thousands of more experienced warriors?

David stood his ground against Saul's doubts by explaining his greatest battle, the source of his warrior confidence.

> ***But David said to Saul, "Your servant has been keeping his father's sheep. When a lion or a bear came and carried off a sheep from the flock, I went after it, struck it and rescued the sheep from its mouth. When it turned on me, I seized it by its hair, struck it and killed it. Your servant has killed both the lion and the bear; this uncircumcised Philistine will be like one of them, because he has defied the armies of the living God."***
>
> 1 Samuel 17:34-36

David presented a unique perspective. Could you do that? Fortunately, there is no need to prove your courage by jumping into the lion cage at the nearest zoo. We can use David's fight with wild animals to showcase the three fundamental weapons of emotion you will need to face any untamed sports giant.

## Warrior's Confidence

In pre-game interviews, players and coaches always seem to embrace the elevated level of team confidence required to assure victory. That injection of courage often comes after a big play or a big fourth-quarter turnover that changed the game's momentum. Athletes will simply state that the close win has given them a renewed sense of confidence going into the next game.

Similarly, David forged his weapon of confidence by calling on previous life-and-death conflicts. David stored up these mental images and the story behind his previous accomplishments as ammo in his armory. The Bible does not mention all the trophies that decorated the walls of David's hunting warehouse, but I am sure that his first adventures with the sling resulted in nailing several smaller predators.

Once target practice on the little guys was over, David stepped up his game by killing the lion and the bear. It was all part of God's plan to make sure David got it right. As God's representative, David would need those previous victories as ammo for his weapon of confidence. The experience of killing a wild animal with his bare hands would have made David's warrior heart overflow with emotion. To have it happen not once, but twice, meant that David had all the ammo he needed to take down the mighty Goliath:

***This uncircumcised Philistine will be like one of them.***

1 Samuel 17:36

Are you like David, a warrior who leads with a passionate heart—then upgrade past experiences by visualizing yourself playing with a tenacious attitude? This is one of the best ways to build up your courage when facing your personal

Goliath. Know, however, that simply watching a great game play out in the theater of your mind is not enough to ensure victory.

It is true that confidence is a powerful emotion that motivates the heart; however, it's not a substitute for preparation. To have the confidence to play your greatest game ever, you must also consider the needs of the mind as well. Feeding the mind with answers will help solve your next test. For athletes, this is not a written test but a visual test in reading and reacting to offensive or defensive schemes. This means we are back to sports tag basics. Building the mind's confidence requires some strategizing to identify which skills will neutralize your opponent's strengths and then combine those skills with a competitive attitude.

In David's case, he didn't need a detailed game plan to fight Goliath. His strategy was simple: kill or be killed. To take Goliath down, David had to choose the right weapon that could target the only vulnerable spot in his body armor. To knock him out, David would have to hit a small opening in Goliath's helmet. To do so would not only require the strength and accuracy of heart and mind but would also require his total confidence in a greater power. Once again, David put his faith in God to deliver him, just as in previous battles. Such strong faith comes from doing and from hearing.

I'm sure David retold his face-to-face encounter with the lion and the bear hundreds of times at family gatherings. In retelling the story over and over, David mentally refined his hunting skills and transformed his confidence into a powerful weapon.

By the time David faced Goliath, his heart, mind, and even his soul had unified their strengths. Armed with only five stones in a life-or-death scenario with Goliath, confidence would not be David's only weapon of emotion.

## Chapter 4

# Aggressiveness

Let's take your weapon of confidence to the next level by adding its partner in punishment. When big jobs require a physical one-two punch, it is time to lock and load an aggressive attitude. In David's case, it takes a certain reckless aggressiveness to go after a wild animal, especially one that sees you as lunch. David talked about this type of attitude when he said:

***When it turned on me, I seized it by its hair ...*** 1 Samuel 17:35

Anytime you seize something, you do it forcefully, especially when you are crazy enough to pull a tiger by his tail. Can you feel David's aggressive attitude when facing a deadly and powerful wild animal? In sports, where does this attitude of aggressiveness come from?

Hall of Fame hockey player Bobby Hull was known for his aggressive playing style that resulted in blinding speed and a feared slap shot. His pre-game ritual started in the locker room where he would sit on the bench and mentally play out an entire hockey game. It was as if he were wearing a virtual reality headset. His mental game was so intense and so physical that he would leave a puddle of sweat on the locker room floor before stepping on the ice.

Using this same process to prepare the military base for action, many athletes just end up creating a nervous sweat. But not Bobby Hull. Playing in 1,063 games in the NHL, his aggressive sweat produced 610 goals, 640 penalty minutes (from loading up too much aggressive firepower), and a Stanley Cup Championship.

Bobby Hull had stumbled onto one of the secrets to creating pre-game aggressiveness. He loaded up his sports warehouse with scoring opportunities that were both real and physical. The ability to picture aggressive game situations can transform an average performance to maximum intensity. When was the last time your mental game generated enough emotion to produce an aggressive sweat?

## Possessiveness

Now, let's look at the most valuable weapon in your arsenal. David's fight with the lion and bear started when they carried off one of his sheep. David spent so much time tending his father's sheep that he could count them in his sleep. His job was to protect the animals from harm and help put food on the family table. So, it was only natural that he became very protective of the sheep under his care. The lion and the bear didn't go after David; David went after *them*. David's possessiveness was the game-changer that motivated him to pick a fight to the death. This protective passion also extended to God and country as well. Goliath mocked the Israelites' God as small and weak. These words triggered a protective desire in David to step up and lead his fellow warriors, no matter the cost.

> ***David asked the men standing near him ... "Who is this uncircumcised Philistine that he should defy the armies of the living God?"*** 1 Samuel 17:26

After a tough loss, coaches are quick to place the blame on turnovers, which are often caused by a lack of possessiveness. Giving up the football creates a huge swing in momentum. The NFL highlights the impact of this mental blunder by tracking the statistics of points scored after a turnover. A positive turnover ratio significantly improves the odds of winning close games.

Possessiveness and protectiveness are intertwined emotions. A lack of protectiveness can cause an offensive player to give up the ball. He or she must become more protective to avoid a repeat performance. For the defense that forced the turnover, these feats are the result of a possessive attitude, one that is constantly seeking to gain ownership of the ball.

Possessiveness is one of the least-used weapons in your arsenal and the most influential in achieving dominance. It's like being injected with a hormonal dose of confidence and aggressiveness right into your veins. Even when you make a multitude of miscalculations—possessiveness is a large-caliber emotion that can find the target.

When a quarterback throws a pass into double coverage, he may be confident, but he lacks a protective attitude. If he had properly loaded his weapon of possessiveness, he would not throw the ball into a dangerous situation. When a blitzing linebacker flies by a stationary quarterback without adjusting to make the tackle, though he is in the aggressive zone, he needs possessiveness to react to the situation and make the sack.

When your weapon of possessiveness is properly loaded, you have weaponized a triple threat of emotion. The combined forces of possessiveness, confidence, and aggressiveness will multiply your firepower to conquer any competitive situation. But possessiveness is an elusive emotion, and it's the toughest weapon to consistently lock and load. How can you maintain a possessive attitude? Once again, at the risk of being redundant, even a simple story can bring powerful emotions to life. Or, if it makes more sense to flip the script—behind every weaponized emotion is a captivating story.

Suppose that the guest speaker at a sports seminar you are attending happens to be your favorite football hero from your beloved NFL team. He has no idea who you are and that you have followed his career and worn his official jersey since preschool. After the program ends, you get the chance to meet him. The shared conversation is great, and to make the day perfect, your sports hero autographs a brand-new football and personalizes it with your name. This ball becomes your cherished possession. It is so valuable that you build a special shrine at home to display and protect it.

One day, you and your best friend, a close teammate, decide to play a little catch in the front yard with your prized possession. Out of nowhere, a couple of guys walking down the street take the ball away and start playing "keep away" from you and your friend. During this confrontation, you learn they are competitors from the team you will face in the upcoming game. Even when you explain that this ball is special, personally autographed, they keep ignoring your request to surrender the ball.

Then one of them finally stops and looks at the ball and says, "Well look at that, there is a funny name on this football." He then spits on it, laughs, and says, "If you want it so bad, come and get it!" By now, his taunting has pulled the pin on the word grenade of disrespect and your heart is ready to explode. He has something that belongs to you, and your subliminal attitude of possessiveness is screaming for you to act—*now*. No need to negotiate any longer; go and get what is rightfully yours!

Why would the football in this story inspire a competitive passion, when any other football means nothing? It is because the ball has been tagged with real ink and has a real story behind it. That changes everything. Now it's personal. It has become your prized possession, and it's your responsibility to protect it. Anytime something is imprinted with your name, a sense of ownership and a mental image of the item is etched inside your brain. When the item is sports-related, you have created a *sports tattoo*.

I'm sure you have heard the phrase, "A picture is worth a thousand words." When a sports tattoo is done right, its image can tell more than a story. It can initialize a host of impressive skills that appeal to a logical mind and bring out a full range of emotions for a competitive heart.

## Chapter 4

How does your name trigger an improved skill-set? Any-time you physically tag a real football, basketball, etc., your mental picture of it is now magnified compared to a regular football you use during practice. Its image has grown to accommodate the story behind it and any sports information attached to it. Now, whenever you see a ball tattooed with your name on it, it triggers a higher level of emotional intensity that activates your hunting mode, better known as "beast mode." When given the command to take back or protect what is yours, all the buildings in your military base are at full alert and combat-ready.

### Time for You to Own It!

When you are trying to maintain ball security or create possessiveness, you are not going to sign your name on all the game balls. Instead, you must mentally generate a sports tattoo as part of your pre-game program.

Start this process by creating a possessive sports tattoo that mentally autographs the ball. You might want to substitute your jersey number for your name to create an emotional bond. Next, mentally label the football with "word grenades." These are self-coaching phrases that cause an explosive change in attitude. Any short narrative that changes hearts and minds can be called a word grenade, even if it's only one sentence. Such phrases as "This ball is mine" or "You will never pry it loose" will detonate a possessive attitude. These word grenades are powerful weapons, so add them to your arsenal. Repeat these descriptive phrases with your inner voice to fire up the heart and mind's protective passion and get back in the game.

Make it personal by adding a storyline of how you paid for that ball with hard work and sweat. Then inject that new emotion along with a signature tattoo into predictable game situations. Now, when someone attempts to take your treasure away, you will guard your prized possession with a protective attitude. Or, if the ball is in the hands of your opponent, you will attack it with a possessive intensity—to take back what is rightfully yours.

If you miss turnover opportunities during the game, then you may need to carry several types of weaponized mantras to trigger a possessive behavior. Use a phrase such as "You have something that belongs to me" or "I worked too hard to let you take what's mine."

If a sports tattoo contains very little emotional attachment, distractions can make it wear off too soon. In the blink of an eye, mentally rubber-stamp your name on the football before the play starts. Reinforce that stamp with a powerful affirmation to target your weapon of possessiveness and to prepare to get the ball back.

The same holds true if you are responsible for giving up the ball. Take time to restore your self-confidence and regain your protectiveness by renewing personal ties to the ball. Repeating a weaponized phrase of possessiveness with your head voice, such as "That ball is all mine and nobody else's" will blow up the self-doubt and help to refocus the power of your head and heart on what matters most.

There is a bonus for a defensive player who has tattooed the ball with an image and uses these simple phrases. You don't have to see the actual ball to experience an explosive transformation in performance. We often see this behavior in dogs. Almost any dog will instinctively attach a word grenade to a four-legged rodent. When the owner shouts the word **"Squirrel!"** it's like pulling the grenade's pin. The explosion can transform even a calm and friendly old dog into a window-banging, bark-his-head-off, hunting machine. That one special word can instantly engage a "mad dog attitude" without even seeing the image of a squirrel. He is only anticipating that one will be found. The lazy dog has become a *Warrior Dog* with a possessive attitude to protect his turf, and there is no way to stop him until nap time intervenes.

Possessive word grenades can be powerful weapons if you keep them clean and positive. In the locker room and during games, you will hear more colorful language, but uncontrolled anger does not put points on the scoreboard or invite God's assistance. It usually results in penalties for taunting or unsportsmanlike conduct—not a smart move when those penalties help swing the game's momentum.

When Dennis Rodman played for the Chicago Bulls, he was known for both his rebounding abilities and his colorful self-expression both on and off the court. During a break in the action, he was caught on camera talking to the basketball. He was convinced that it was ignoring him. When he called its name, it didn't respond by coming to him. With Dennis' ever-changing choice of hair color (which includes a rainbow design), numerous tattoos, piercings, and a flamboyant behavior (he wore a white wedding dress to marry himself), no one was surprised at his verbal confrontation with the basketball.

This ball-talking behavior, however, does offer a unique perspective on how to connect with an inanimate object. In Dennis Rodman's mind, the ball was alive and even had a name. People sometimes name and even talk to their cars and their musical instruments, but Rodman was attempting to modify the ball's behavior. Was he hoping it would respond like a personal pet, close friend, or a bouncy new bride? We don't know, but his heartfelt connection created a very possessive attitude.

## Momma Bear Love

Imagine yourself standing on the pier at your neighbor's pond watching your little brother swim. You notice an alligator slip into the water at one end of the pond and see it heading right for your brother. After you jump up and down and scream at the top of your lungs, your brother realizes the danger and swims frantically towards the pier. As the alligator closes the gap, you realize that your brother is not going to make it, so you yell, "Give me your hand!"

Just as you grab hold of your brother's arm, the alligator clamps down on his swim fin and won't let go. Your brother is trapped in a life-and-death tug of war. The fear in his eyes triggers the thought "He is my brother; he is mine." Then every muscle in your body is energized to squeeze even tighter. Your heart races and your fingernails dig into the boy's skin until blood appears. The moment seems to last forever... but suddenly something causes the alligator to let go. Maybe it was tired or didn't like the taste of the rubber fin. But from that day on, whenever anyone asks about the scars on your little bother's arm, you smile and say, "Those are love scars, from an unstoppable love."

It's not nice to play games with your heart, but which style creates a possessive attitude for you? If you have already named your bike, car, or musical instrument, then it's only natural to name the ball to make it personal. Or would you prefer to use a human storyline with momma-bear courage to channel a feeling of possessiveness? Either of these methods will load powerful weapons of emotion and keep a target on the game ball.

Tagging the football with a possessive tattoo will not work for every position or in every sport. Kickers in the NFL want to boot the ball as far as possible. They are all about distance and accuracy, not possessiveness. When lining up to kick an extra point or field goal, it's common for kickers to target a noticeable fan whose seat lines up between the goalposts and say, "This one's for you!" In baseball, hitting a home run means giving the ball away to someone in the grandstands. In these situations, tagging the ball with a personalized autograph may require a unique emotion. Perhaps an aggressive generosity will improve accuracy.

Right before a game starts, most athletes have their own version of Goliath doubt. If that happens to you, commit to silencing that provoking little head voice. You might not picture your demons as a little giant with bulging baby muscles, but the closer to game time, the louder his harassing words will echo throughout the base of military operations. Doubt can rattle your nerves, knot up your stomach, and cause crippling confusion throughout the military base. You can regain control by trusting God and having an arsenal filled with his weapons. Have you taken the time to load his weapons of confidence, aggressiveness, and possessiveness?

## A Heart-Driven Gladiator

Before the death match with Goliath, David's battles in defeating the lion and the bear involved basic hunting skills and leading with a fearless heart. When his heart took control, he ignored any conventional wisdom implying the risk of failure or death.

When the commanding officers of the Israelite army saw David enter the battlefield, they had to admire his courage but wonder about his sanity. How could fighting the mighty Goliath without wearing body armor or even carrying a sword become a winning strategy? Then hearing David, armed without a sword but with a staff and sling, claim, "I'll strike you down and cut off your head," would have raised even more doubt about his state of mind.

David's taunting words to Goliath illustrate the truth Jesus spoke in Luke 6:45: "For the mouth speaks what his heart is full of." Once again, the emotional reservoir in David's heart had reached its limit. His previous combat experience was defined by slaying the lion and the bear, and Goliath would be like one of them. The epic battle was not about conventional wisdom but about weapons of emotion and believing in a power greater than himself—God.

## Confidence Clinic

Confidence, aggressiveness, and possessiveness are powerful weapons that everyone should own, especially athletes.

Although possessiveness is a very elusive emotion, holding on to your confidence will be one of your greatest challenges. The Bible makes this warning with a promise.

***So do not throw away your confidence; it will be richly rewarded.***
Hebrews 10:35

This biblical principle is about a heavenly reward, but let's apply it to the real world. Someone with military training would never willingly let go of a real weapon during a battle and be defenseless. Yet, how many times have you seen pro athletes get mad and lose their confidence? Confidence is not always something you build up. Many times you have plenty of confidence to do the job, until you give it up and replace it with some type of fear or doubt. As soon as you or your team's confidence is considered dead, the other team is more than happy to put the nail in the coffin. Besides, giving up doesn't win the close games. However, fighting to the end while firmly holding on to your courage and confidence does, and the reward is priceless.

Let's review techniques pro athletes use to build their confidence and see if we can build the type of rock-solid confidence that no one can steal. Our efforts started with LeBron saying, "My mind is my most powerful weapon!" How did LeBron transform his *mind* into a weapon of confidence? His strategy utilized logic to sort through the confusion. Sports tags helped him to mentally organize what his mind wanted to execute, and his heart joined the fight. Jerry Rice was next with his method of using repetition to run plays over and over in the theater of his mind. This process of using repetition convinced his over-emotional *heart* that every play was doable and had nothing to worry about. And, as mentioned, David forged his weapon of unshakable confidence from his deadly encounters with wild animals. David's experience created a storyline where he knew God was fighting by his side and provided the *spiritual* connection needed to transform his fears into confidence.

If you struggle with the problem of not holding onto your confidence, then review how these three warriors eliminated the issues of a timid head, heart, and soul. Their weapons of confidence were customized to satisfy the dominant part of their psyche. When it comes to improving your confidence, which one of the three entities is not up to speed or holding you back? Does your heart desire an emotional boost? Is the head requesting a logical game plan, or is your soul craving a spiritual connection to something greater? Now that you know the secrets of top athletes, it's time to fill your arsenal with what you need to sustain a high level of confidence. Once it's stocked with weapons customized to fit your hand, nothing can convince you to throw them away.

I'm sure you have heard coaches talk about character building and how those strengths can carry over from sports into real life. But what does God consider the most important life lesson in sports? *Perseverance!* That means sticking with the game plan and his game plan calls for you to be resilient both on and off the field. He wants you to have the skills and self-assurance to bounce back from any type of adversity. The following is how God strengthens your character regardless of the outcome.

> ***Consider it pure joy, my brothers and sisters, whenever you face trials of many kinds, because you know that the testing of your faith produces perseverance. Let perseverance finish its work so that you may be mature and complete, not lacking anything.***
>
> James 1:2-4

God's goal is for you to be a warrior who is mature and complete, not lacking "anything," including an arsenal filled with his unstoppable weapons. He wants you to develop that unique quality called *perseverance*. It is common to strive for perfection, but perfection can be your enemy. In reality, no one's stats stay at 100% for very long. Even one small mistake in trying to achieve a perfect game can break your will to succeed and stop you dead in your tracks. The driving force winners seek is perseverance. It never admits defeat or throws in the towel when your confidence is being tested.

When the going gets tough, the tendency is to anticipate a future filled with grief and trying situations. Yet, God sees the big picture. Your next challenge is God's way of testing your courage. Now that we have uncovered a number of weapons David used to face his Goliath, have you changed your perspective? Are your weapons of emotion ready for battle? Your ability to persevere, while still holding onto your confidence will reveal the depth of your sports armory and expose which weapons you may be lacking.

# God's Boot Camp

## Chapter 5

Every great athlete and every great warrior goes through some type of specialized training program. Could young David be the exception when he went one-on-one with Goliath? It would appear probable. David was a shepherd boy, and shepherds do not receive formal training to become elite soldiers. But somehow King Saul looked past David's job title and the invincible teenage attitude to see the heart of a real warrior. How did David seal the deal and become the number-one pick to fight the giant Goliath? It all happened when King Saul heard David talk about his boot camp experience:

> ***"The LORD who rescued me from the paw of the lion and the paw of the bear will rescue me from the hand of this Philistine."***
>
> 1 Samuel 17:37

King Saul recognized that David had found that "something extra" that made a game-changing difference. David's beliefs were more powerful than lucky clothing and rituals. David's faith in God would feed his spiritual entity—the soul and give him a huge advantage to fight beyond himself. David had filled his mental warehouse with the type of faith that would disarm his doubts and combat his fears when facing the mighty Goliath.

David's confidence was built from a type of warrior training that Saul could never offer his troops. The king's training was nowhere near as tough or dangerous as the "on the job" training David had faced, nor did it offer a spiritual connection with the God who is powerful enough to command the universe.

David's relationship with God and his experience of being repeatedly delivered by the Lord convinced the king that David would be victorious. That is why...

> ***... Saul said to David, "Go, and the Lord be with you."*** 1 Samuel 17:37

These are powerful words, like sweet music to quicken the warrior's heart: Prepare for combat! David had received his marching orders, confirmation that he would represent an army of thousands. King Saul's words had established David as a warrior, and God was ready to fight at his side. So what does God say to nervous warriors and fearful athletes before they go into battle?

> ***"Have I not commanded you? Be strong and courageous. Do not be afraid; do not be discouraged, for the Lord your God will be with you wherever you go."*** Joshua 1:9

Doesn't that sound like the type of leadership you would expect from a commanding officer addressing new recruits? These are powerful words of encouragement indicating that boot camp was over. The next step to becoming a true warrior would take place on the battlefield. God was reassuring the troops that even with limited combat experience, they were expected to persevere. And, they were not meant to fight alone; God will always be by their side, fighting with them to protect his kingdom.

All of us, not just athletes, are called to be kingdom minded. But how can anyone run a military base to protect God's kingdom without first going through basic training?

Let's look at how God's plan for David played out.

The final phase of David's warrior training had now concluded. David had gone head-to-head with vicious wild beasts. His graduation from God's boot camp was complete. With enough points to become a Top Gun graduate, he would be allowed to face the giant Goliath. Years later, David's experience would be written down in a song acknowledging God's continued on-the-job training.

> ***For who is God besides the Lord?***
> ***And who is the Rock except our God?***
> ***It is God who arms me with strength***
> ***and makes my way secure.***
> ***He makes my feet like the feet of a deer;***
> ***he causes me to stand on the heights.***
> ***He trains my hands for battle;***
> ***my arms can bend a bow of bronze.***
> ***You make your saving help my shield;***
> ***Your help has made me great.***
> ***You provide a broad path for my feet,***
> ***so that my ankles do not give way.***
> 2 Samuel 22:32-37

If your coaches drop the wind sprints and have you chasing deer ... if weight lifting is replaced by bronze-bow bending ... and if tackling drills have become hand-to-hand combat maneuvers, there may be a higher power at work. It could be part of God's design to upgrade your boot camp training.

The beauty of God's basic training is that these skills eventually helped David become a great king. The journey that led David to be the best warrior he could be, began in the fields as he tended his flock of sheep. Although he was lacking in normal weapons, David was mentally prepared with confidence, aggressiveness, and a very protective attitude to defend the lives and integrity of God's army. David was also expecting God to show up in a big way with the encouragement and leadership that was bigger than any lucky charm, delivering him once again from his enemy.

## God's Many Faces

Given the popularity of the David and Goliath story, why don't we hear more about God's existence on the battlefield? David called him the "God of the living armies." God also took the role of a commander-in-chief by personally directing numerous battles recorded in the Old Testament. With all the biblical military victories, it makes you wonder why God's military face is missing from Sunday morning sermons.

The first time I heard about God as a military leader and soldier on the battlefield was at the men's group at our church. One of the sessions on godly manhood touched on the subject of *God as a warrior*, and it opened my eyes. Though I connected with that perspective in a new way, my newfound revelation only received a *what-in-the-world* look from my wife.

God's leadership as a military mastermind is something Bible experts have recognized for some time. God's "warrior" title first appears in Exodus chapter 15, where he starts a personal battle with Pharaoh's army and disposes of all the soldiers in short order. During this battle, Moses identifies God by declaring:

***The LORD is a warrior.***

Exodus 15:3

The story describes how God's warrior face showed up just in time to save his chosen people on their way to the Promised Land. The Israelites were untouched as God the warrior used his weapons of mass destruction to destroy the Egyptian army marching in hot pursuit.

Besides God's many faces, God also uses many different names to identify and reveal the different characteristics of his personality. These names and faces are used according to the varying roles God plays to achieve his plan.

After God's battle with Pharaoh's army, you would think that the Israelites would be calling God the great *Warrior*. Instead, they ended up using a name that is of great interest to athletes—"Yahweh." Not only is "Yahweh" a sacred name for God, but it is so holy that out of fear and respect it was not to be spoken out loud. It is also a name so powerful that it was used in reference to God's warrior face.

When the situation calls for God to be your commanding officer, who is also in charge of angel armies, he wants you to be well-armed. He also wants to be a part of your game plan, and he is ready to stand with you in the battle zone. His relationship to you as a fellow soldier is revealed in the Old Testament:

***... With us is Yahweh our God to help us and to fight our battles.***

2 Chronicles 32:8 (WEB)

It is not hard to see the commanding tone in God's word when Yahweh is doing the talking. The most notable verses have very descriptive language concerning what God will do to his enemies.

***All who rage against you will surely be ashamed and disgraced; those who oppose you will be as nothing and perish. Though you search for your enemies, you will not find them. Those who wage war against you will be as nothing at all.***

Isaiah 41:11-12

## Chapter 5

Hearing more about God's warrior face in church services might improve attendance among sports fans, but what does this have to do with you and playing competitive sports? A clue is found in the first book of the Bible:

> ***So God created mankind in his own image, in the image of God he created them; male and female he created them.***
>
> Genesis 1:27

Since you were created in God's image, many of God's faces and attributes are embedded in your DNA. When it comes to sports, there is no hiding God's warrior persona. Everyone knows when God's heart and mind show up to play. To become an authentic warrior means taking on great power and, with it, great responsibilities. This will require understanding the appropriate time and place to wear the face of a warrior, along with keeping it in balance with the other faces that are pleasing to God.

### The Four Faces of Man

Our men's group studied a video series titled *The Quest for Authentic Manhood* by Dr. Robert Lewis. For this series, some of the guys in the group split off to meet on a different night and met in an outbuilding the size of a four-car garage. The leader, the owner of the building, was a craftsman and cabinet maker who used this building to house his commercial-grade woodworking equipment. For those who like the smell of sawdust and power tools, it was a glimpse of Heaven. Even Tim the tool man from the old TV show *Home Improvement* would grunt in approval.

After the weekly video teaching and discussion, we spent time on food and fellowship. The guy-talk ranged from sports to hunting and fishing stories to anything with a motor. It was then that I learned some of the best-kept man secrets.

Besides not stopping for directions, real men never read the instructions in the box. When it comes to man food, I learned that eating real man-chili means you eat what you kill. (To avoid the light-hearted banter, I refrained from disclosing that all my hunting for man-chili was done at the grocery store.)

The *Authentic Manhood* program we used covered the four faces of a man as modeled by Jesus Christ and directed by the Word of God. The four faces are the king, warrior, friend, and lover. This series explains how God created you in his image with the ability to be multi-dimensional. No one wears the same face all the time. When used properly, each face needs to be in balance with the appropriate time and place.

This raises the question of how you perceive God. Do you accept the idea of God wearing a totally different face in sports as in your personal life? When you're more than a spectator, is God your coach, barking out orders like a king commanding his armies? Or is God a warrior, similar to a fellow teammate that will fight by your side? Will your head and heart be inspired or reject either type of relationship?

When I played sports in high school, many of my teammates would stumble awkwardly to wear the right face. Most would display a warrior's aggressive attitude in the locker room *after* a tough loss instead of before the game. A few would show up at game time with a king face that didn't fool anyone. They didn't understand the true leadership skills associated with it. A similar reaction would occur if they wore a friend or a lover face during a heated competition.

Unfortunately, our coach didn't offer any type of leadership program to help athletes step up and inspire fellow teammates. For now, we'll focus on developing your warrior's game face and leave lover boy Romeo, Elvis the king impersonator, and your friendly Forrest Gump personalities cheering on the sideline.

## Chapter 5

In sports, it's a challenge to convince the head and heart to wear the face of a warrior. If the heart feels underappreciated or disrespected, you can count on a half-hearted effort. If the logical mind cannot contribute or connect with the game plan, it may pout as well. If either one of them holds you back, you can end up sitting on the bench wearing the face of a wimp.

In another extreme situation, if either is mad at the world, you can end up with devastating road rage that crosses the line to seek revenge. When you are consumed with the desire to "get even," expect to foul out or be ejected for unsportsmanlike behavior, which only penalizes the entire team. To best understand what God expects from a true warrior, let's look at the story of the centurion in Luke 7:1-10.

Some of the Jewish elders requested that Jesus heal a centurion's servant who was about to die. The elders pleaded with Jesus because the centurion loved Israel and helped build a synagogue. While Jesus traveled to his house, the centurion sent a messenger to say, "Lord, don't trouble yourself, for I do not deserve to have you come under my roof. That is why I did not even consider myself worthy to come to you. But say the word, and my servant will be healed. For I myself am a man under authority, with soldiers under me. I tell this one, 'Go,' and he goes; and that one, 'Come,' and he comes. I say to my servant, 'Do this,' and he does it." Jesus was amazed, and to the crowd following him, he said, "I tell you, I have not found such great faith even in Israel." When the elders returned to the house, the servant had recovered.

The centurion was a Roman soldier whose warrior qualities started with great faith in God. His love for God and Israel inspired him to help with building a synagogue. Even though he was powerful enough to command 100-foot soldiers and rule over the Jews in his territory, he was not about to put himself above Jesus. He understood the meaning of high moral standards and being under the authority of someone else. In sports, all the athletes are under the authority of a coach, the rule book, and, most importantly, the referee.

## God's Private Arsenal

God not only has a warrior's face, but he maintains his own arsenal of weapons. The size of the battle determines the power and number of weapons he chooses.

> ***The LORD has opened his arsenal and brought out the weapons of his wrath, for the Sovereign LORD Almighty has work to do in the land of the Babylonians.***
>
> Jeremiah 50:25

Playing your best requires preparation. Winning requires having the right weapons. When God is your commanding officer, he can supply you with weapons from his arsenal for whatever battle you face. When it comes to impressive weapons, God chose to "stir up the spirit of a destroyer" (Jeremiah 51:1) to deal with the only reigning superpower, Babylonia. As awesome as that sounds, my personal favorite is the angel of death.

Having an angel who would fight for you would be awesome and definitely impress your friends, but don't think you will get your hands on it or any other of God's high-powered weapons of wrath. God knows better than to trust you with 100-pound hailstones when a tough loss might inspire taking out the other team's concession stand. And when a defender makes you look bad, God won't let you retaliate by zapping him or her with lightning bolts.

When it comes to sports, God has weapons in his arsenal designed for mental preparation before and during the game. His strategy is for you to store up these unique weapons in your personal armory. Finding enough weapons to fill your arsenal can be challenging. Just as in the story of David and Goliath, God has hidden these weapons in plain sight.

## A Warrior's Heart

Why are so many people sports fanatics? And why does the Super Bowl have the highest ratings with all demographics, and why has it become the most celebrated sporting event in the world? Could it be because everyone is born with a sports-filled heart? Close, but only half right. Everyone is born with a *warrior's* heart.

Let's face it. Though we all carry emotional ammo from God's arsenal to do battle, not all hearts are triggered in the same way. In dire situations, ladies are surprised at their own ability to show up with momma bear courage and protect their young. Even people who couldn't hurt a flea will rise up with the courage to fight off a blood-thirsty mosquito, while others choose a military career to fight off blood-thirsty terrorists.

In his book *Four Pillars of a Man's Heart*, Stu Weber outlines how to become, like David, a man after God's own heart. To keep everything in balance, a man's heart must have four pillars: a king pillar, a warrior pillar, a mentor pillar, and a friend pillar. Weber does an excellent job of defining a true warrior and what his heart should look like.

> ***If we are utilizing the warrior's heart rightly, we will be energetic, self-sacrificing men, like our Lord. We will be alert, decisive, courageous, loyal, and persevering—all to the greater good of those near and dear to us. We will fight the good fight. And the world will be a better place for it.***
>
> Stu Weber

In sports, the warriors with the biggest, bravest hearts are on the field of play, while teammates on the sidelines are still working to play with more heart. Fellow warriors, if physically unable to compete, have a heartfelt desire to be as close to the battle zone as possible. These big-hearted spectators are willing to withstand bone-chilling temperatures to enjoy great seats at the game, while honorary warriors are content to stay comfortable at home and cheer on their comrades on the TV battlefield.

During the mid-1980s, a bigger-than-life personality appeared in the football world. He was literally so big that his real name, William Perry, was rarely used. He was better known by adoring fans as "Refrigerator Perry" or just "The Fridge."

Fans loved the Fridge's multifaceted attitude off the field. Even with a missing front tooth, his giant infectious smile would shine as brightly as any refrigerator light bulb. On the field, though, it was a different story, as Perry battled with a warrior's heart to stop the run. He soon became a Pro Bowl defensive lineman for the Chicago Bears. Once the Fridge stepped off the sideline onto the football field, you could see his warrior's face come alive; his heart was ready to do battle.

If you have had the opportunity to meet any well-known sports personalities, you may have wondered how these friendly, gentle giants can transform from teddy bears into Tasmanian devils at game time. Now you know! Nobody wears the face of a warrior all the time, but the great athletes know when it's appropriate to power up their military base of operations and prepare for battle.

God has a master game plan for you, an initiative that will involve using all four of your faces. Does your path include being the next king of Israel or perhaps the next King James of the basketball court? Whatever it is, it takes patience to let God's plan play out. God has chosen you to be a part of a life-long journey. Part of that quest may involve sports and learning to wear the face of a warrior. From this competitive experience, the development of your military base can carry over to make an impact in the game of life.

Here's the deal: God is on your side and wants you to enlist in his boot camp. Fortunately, God is not as selective as the armed forces. God will recruit anyone—young and old, short, and tall. Everyone is pre-approved to join God's army. You don't have to do any type of spiritual exercises to get in shape or pretend to be some type of religious person you're not. God wants you just the way you are.

Even with all the miraculous things that Jesus did, his own disciples had their doubts about God's plan. When the angry crowd took Jesus away, the disciples' confidence was shattered as they scattered. Peter, one of the disciples, denied even knowing Jesus, not once but three times. Thomas, another disciple, wouldn't believe that Jesus was resurrected until he put his fingers in Jesus's wounds, thus earning the nickname "Doubting Thomas."

God will accept you as you are. You may have doubts about plugging into God's power as well, but even a small amount of faith can bulldoze a mountain of doubts out of the sports warehouse. So, are you ready to join his army and sign up for his boot camp? Are you prepared to have a commanding officer who will train you to be the best warrior you can be and help you fight the battles against your toughest opponent? David wrote this about his commanding officer:

***The Lord is my strength and my shield;***
***my heart trusts in him, and he helps me.***

Psalm 28:7

It all starts with the hard part—volunteering to take that first step forward to follow his lead. If you still feel like sitting on the sidelines, that's okay, but God wants you in the game and will even supply the weapons for your arsenal. Basic training can begin if you are ready to accept God as your commanding officer who will fight by your side both in sports and in the game of life.

Maybe you feel it is an unfair advantage to tap directly into God's power and have his military skills on your side; he is the commander of angel armies. He has more than enough strength to place the stars in the sky and more than enough power to destroy his enemies, yet, now he is pleased to accept you as his fresh recruit.

## Basic Equipment for Boot Camp

God is all about transformational relationships and developing mutual trust. Boot camp is where it all begins. As trust builds, negative paralysis fades away. Even in sports, mutual trust improves teamwork. Any collaboration starts by being intentional, and a good first step is to listen to your commanding officer's recommendations.

God's not looking to incriminate you with his laws but to give you "rules of the road" for your protection. These rules encourage you to avoid driving too fast for life's weather conditions and teach you how to avoid taking the wrong road. God's laws are meant to bless and protect you, just as guard rails help you avoid life's heart-breaking circumstances.

We need so many fundamental skills to stay on the narrow road of life that God decided we should have a training manual. Maybe it's time to blow the dust off your old Bible. If you do not have one, buy one, preferably a study Bible that sheds extra light on God's game plan.

You may be wondering if a book written thousands of years ago can apply to today's world of competitive sports. Of course it can. The remnants of arenas built during biblical times are still standing as a reminder of popular sporting events. Some featured chariot races, while others were designed for a fight to the death against men and man-eating animals. We have already covered the Apostle Paul's sports analogy about running the race, finishing strong, and winning the prize. Other biblical writers emphasized qualities found in great athletes such as perseverance, resilience, discipline, strength, and courage. It may take some digging to find the Bible verses we can apply to sports-related situations, but many will motivate a warrior's heart and mind.

God wants to transform you into a better warrior now. To ensure that the right type of training is taking place, the Bible has numerous warrior stories just for you. These Bible verses can guide you in coaching the head and heart as you develop a pre-game program. See if you can highlight verses that might make your top-10 playlist as pre-game favorites. Such warrior verses can confirm a powerful relationship between God, your commander-in-chief, and you as his enlisted warrior.

But be forewarned: just as God's spiritual forces are working to bless you, evil forces are waiting to take you down. Expect serious spiritual warfare when you try to expand God's kingdom—even inside your own mind. If you're brave enough to venture just outside the walls of your comfort zone, there is danger lurking nearby, waiting to consume your efforts.

***Be alert and of sober mind. Your enemy the devil prowls around like a roaring lion looking for someone to devour.*** 1 Peter 5:8

This is the typical game plan for the devil. If a trash-talking giant isn't standing in your way, then it's someone impersonating a loud-mouth lion. Any lion that makes its presence known with a loud roar is not trying to sneak up on you but to scare you to death. He has the ferocity to overwhelm your confidence so you will turn-tail and run.

Regardless of how threatening your demons appear to be, their efforts to call your bluff are an attempt to devour what little is left of your confidence. They know that once you start backing down, you have no chance of completing the mission and receiving God's greater reward.

Great teams that make it to the playoffs have athletes who are willing to step up and become great leaders regardless of their teammates' performance. The worldly approach to becoming a leader is to go it alone, do it your way, and not depend on anyone. Let go of this illusion of doing everything on your own. The pursuit of authentic leadership originates from having a higher power as your mentor. God can be your coach on speed dial for guidance and support. He knows all about the issues of the heart and mind, and the right way to run a military base. God's help can be the catalyst for becoming the leader your teammates turn to for renewed confidence ... especially when the team's scoring momentum has hit a stone wall of fear.

God's plan is simple. Boot camp is about facing your biggest fears and depending on God's help to conquer those fears. Each time a biblical leader's faith was tested, he grew closer to God and learned how to persevere through seemingly unbearable circumstances. Those who graduated were changed from the inside out. They became a whole lot tougher than they thought and received a deeper understanding and respect for God's unbelievable power.

Don't think that you can just sign up and start walking on water. There are no shortcuts when it comes to God's training programs. David started his boot camp experience by fighting small animals. His self-confidence and faith in God gradually grew until he was ready to fight the lion and the bear. All these battles gave him the training and the courage to fight the giant Goliath. It is no mistake when God uses previous battles in your life as stepping stones to grow your warrior's heart and improve your leadership skills.

Developing leadership skills takes time. When you look

at the great leaders in the Bible, one of the common themes is that God takes an unlikely, unqualified character and leads him on a path through an unconventional boot camp. For some reason it often takes 40 days to complete God's game plan. When Noah was in the ark, it rained for 40 days. Moses was on the mountain for 40 days before receiving the Ten Commandments and Goliath did 40 days' worth of trash-talking to rattle the confidence of the Israeli army. Even God's own Son experienced 40 days of wilderness survival training. During that time, the devil tried every trick in the book to destroy his confidence in God's plan. Instead of giving up, Jesus remained totally dependent on God for both his physical and spiritual needs.

When your heart, mind, and soul have what they need to feel confident, no one can take that away; not Goliath, not a roaring lion, not even your toughest critics have that kind of power over you. But that won't stop the devil from using people and unpredictable situations to mess with your game. Will you let him succeed? You see, it's still your decision, your call, whether to keep your confidence intact or throw it out the front door of the sports warehouse.

If your leadership skills are on a roller coaster, take the "40-Day Leadership Challenge." The goal is to do an extreme remodeling job on your mental warehouse. It takes a 40-day project to build your confidence into a permanent fixture. Just start each morning with the promise found in Hebrews 10:35, "So do not throw away your confidence; it will be richly rewarded." Follow it up with a positive affirmation to use throughout the day, such as, "I will hold onto my confidence." Add some possessiveness to your mantra by anticipating who or what circumstance will attempt to knock you down. Include ways to fight back, such as standing your ground with the truth or maintaining your composure in a hostile unpredictable situation.

Most guys have no idea of the power that comes from holding on to God's transformational promises. If you are committed to marking 40 days off the calendar, you will notice a surge in your confidence long before completion. You will be kicking that roaring lion out of your life with its tail between its legs. No longer will you let fear win the day.

After successfully completing the 40-Day Leadership Challenge, carry the following "confidence card" with you. When the competition pushes you to the limit, it can be used as a mental reminder of your ability to persevere. This card is the definition of authentic leadership based on Hebrews 10:35.

*COPY ON HEAVY CARD STOCK*
*CUT OUT AND ATTACH BACK-TO-BACK*

As a *Leader I* will hold onto my confidence to:

- *Face Trials of Many Kinds*
- *Accept Responsibility*
- *Reject Fear and Doubt*
- *Develop Perseverance*
- *Expect a Greater Reward*

*God's Leadership Promise*

***So do not throw away your confidence; it will be richly rewarded.***
*Hebrews 10:35*

***God's Sports Arsenal***

# God's Sports Arsenal

## Chapter 6

The search to fill your arsenal with some of God's divine weapons began with the story of David and Goliath. There we found three weapons of emotion: confidence, aggressiveness, and possessiveness. They served to unify David's heart, mind, and soul, but God's arsenal contains so much more. Some of my personal favorites, besides the angel of death and the spirit of a destroyer, include flaming arrows, earthquakes, hailstones, a flamethrower that can melt mountains like wax, and the equivalent of a nuclear warhead that leveled the cities of Sodom and Gomorrah. Fortunately, none of these weapons are destined for use by the unstable human race. But, what about God's weapons that we humans *can* use?

The most famous weapon God gave to his people was the Ark of the Covenant. It possessed "radioactive" energy that could burn or kill those who touched it. It could weaken the structural integrity in the walls of Jericho until they collapsed, and it could multiply the rat population while spreading tumors to every person in the city. But don't worry, according to Indiana Jones, it is safely locked away in a secret government warehouse.

The biblical stories of God's weapons of wrath make for insightful reading. Though these weapons reveal God's unequaled military power and strategic mind, they are off-limits for competitive sports. God does have weapons in his arsenal, however, that are better suited for improving athletic performance.

### Dress for a Military Success

Consider your next game a test of courage. To help weaponize your mindset and protect your warrior's heart, your arsenal should include a set of the finest multi-threat resistant body armor. Fortunately, God has warehoused extra sets that are just your size. Before starting your tour of duty, the Apostle Paul instructs you to develop your inner warrior. Make it a daily ritual to wear the armor of God because no one knows when your demons will show up. They would love to knock you down and steal your confidence, so be prepared to "stand your ground."

> ***Therefore put on the full armor of God, so that when the day of evil comes, you may be able to stand your ground, and after you have done everything, to stand. Stand firm then, with the belt of truth buckled around your waist, with the breastplate of righteousness in place, and with your feet fitted with the readiness that comes from the gospel of peace. In addition to all this, take up the shield of faith, with which you can extinguish all the flaming arrows of the evil one. Take the helmet of salvation and the sword of the Spirit, which is the word of God.***
>
> Ephesians 6:13-17

Notice that the sword is the only offensive weapon used in spiritual warfare. The other components of God's armor are for defensive purposes. We are called not only to defend but, when our relationship with God is under attack, to pick up the sword (God's word) and go on the offensive. Judging by God's choice of the sword, as opposed to a bow or sling, the combat is up close and personal. We must attain a true victory using the sheer knowledge and power of God's word and not negotiating or compromising our faith.

Paul, aware of Roman soldiers' gear, used this military terminology to relate to Christ-followers in a whole new way.

Since they lived in Ephesus, a large city rife with idol worship, sorcery, illicit sex, and foolish philosophies, life would be a battle. When Paul describes each piece of God's armor, it is all about setting up as many mental pathways as possible so the head and heart can work together. He is combining the *passionate* mindset of a soldier with biblical coaching instructions to create a powerful spiritual tag. These divinely inspired images would motivate his readers to wear the face of a warrior and hold onto their spiritual confidence when facing various moral and spiritual foes. The obvious question is, "How can we utilize God's body armor in sports battles?"

During biblical times, a military belt was commonly used to hold everything together. Its function was to tie down the breastplate, keep loose clothing in place, and hold extra weapons of war. In Ephesians 6, the "belt of truth" symbolizes keeping your life together with the truth of God's promises. Think of it as avoiding a wardrobe malfunction. If you are living a lie or even telling one, everything in your life can come undone and be as embarrassing as being caught with your pants down. You cannot run from a lie when things start falling apart.

The "breastplate of righteousness" not only symbolizes God's goodness and doing what is right in God's eyes but also acts as a multi-threat resistant vest. The enemy is aiming at your warrior's heart, and God's righteousness will protect you from being pierced by a sword or arrow of evil influences.

Being accompanied by the "gospel of peace" means carrying the good news of the kingdom. That peace will come with a call to action, to be ready to share the good news. In sports, it is critical to have "your feet fitted with the readiness" to face any competitive situation. When your number is called, your marching orders are to jump off the bench and execute God's game plan.

Taking the "helmet of salvation" symbolizes protecting your vulnerable head as well as your brain from any fatal blows. In competitive sports you will be knocked around as other athletes, coaches, and even the sports media attempt to rattle your faith with temptations to disobey God. The closer you get to God, the more head-butts you will receive. Without a spiritual helmet for protection, these battles can cloud your decisions in sports and in life or even blur the true path to Heaven.

The last defensive piece of armor is the "shield of faith," which is the first line of defense. Faith involves a huge element of trust. You must hold on to your faith and, in this case, use it to extinguish all the flaming arrows of the evil one. Flaming arrows include any type of situation that shakes your faith with a heightened sense of fear and anxiety. During biblical times, everyone could relate to the words, "They have flaming arrows!" The thought of becoming a human fireball can be unnerving.

Today, consider the flaming arrows as word grenades that detonate during a game and are responsible for huge changes in momentum. These flaming arrows create fear, doubt, and hesitation. When your best athlete (the big playmaker) has gone down with an injury, the team's confidence can be destroyed just as fast as the Philistine army's confidence when Goliath was knocked out cold. When turnovers turn into points on the scoreboard, it can be a confidence builder or a flaming arrow, depending on which side you are on. It's up to you to "take up the shield of faith" when the arrows of doubt are flying, and the word grenades are being launched. With God's help to extinguish the emotional burn, you can continue to fight against impossible odds towards victory.

***The LORD is my rock, my fortress and my deliverer; my God is my rock, in whom I take refuge, my shield and the horn of my salvation, my stronghold.*** Psalm 18:2

Who had the greatest shield of faith in Israel? The same centurion in Luke 7:1-10 we met in the last chapter. The Roman soldier understood the chain of command and didn't consider himself worthy of having Jesus come to his house to heal his servant. The centurion's great faith acknowledged that Jesus had the authority to simply give the order and the healing would be carried out. When Jesus heard the centurion's words of faith, Jesus was astonished and said to those following him, "I tell you the truth, I have not found anyone in Israel with such great faith."

## Swords from the Spirit

In the first chapter, we found LeBron saying that his mind is his most powerful weapon, and we were left to imagine what that weapon might look like. The Bible, however, doesn't leave you guessing, but defines your most powerful weapon as a "sword of the Spirit." When you need to wear the face of a warrior, it provides that "something extra." It can be a hands-on experience that will trigger the feeling of being armed and confident, ready for any situation.

God's sword is not only a weapon capable of protecting your spiritual entity, but is endorsed as God's weapon of choice when he appears in the physical form of a military commander. (Joshua 5:13-14, Revelation 19:15) Even the angels in God's army carry a sword. (Numbers 22:31)

The multi-threat-resistant body armor that God wants you to wear is already tagged with logic and emotion. When it comes to the sword of the Spirit, however, this formidable weapon is shrouded in mystery.

Christians commonly believe that the entire Bible represents the sword of the Spirit. The scriptures do contain many appeals to fight the everyday battles in life, but not every verse can be weaponized to transform hearts and minds. When Jesus said to look at the lilies of the field in

Matthew chapter 6, was he thinking a flower sword can help you to wear the face of a warrior? Of course not!

We already have scripture that defines the gifts of the Spirit and fruits of the Spirit, but what about the "Swords of the Spirit"? Since the Bible doesn't list the Spirit's swords and their application, we must search for the verses that apply to sports. The Apostle Paul writes a great definition of the type of weapons we need.

***The weapons we fight with are not the weapons of the world. On the contrary, they have divine power to demolish strongholds.***

2 Corinthians 10:4

Paul confirms the concept of having a personal arsenal with multiple weapons at your disposal. And, the weapons "you fight with" are defined as having divine power, enough to do some serious damage. Does this sound like the type of weapons worth searching for? To get you started, let's look at a few basic swords of the Spirit recommended for any athlete in any sport.

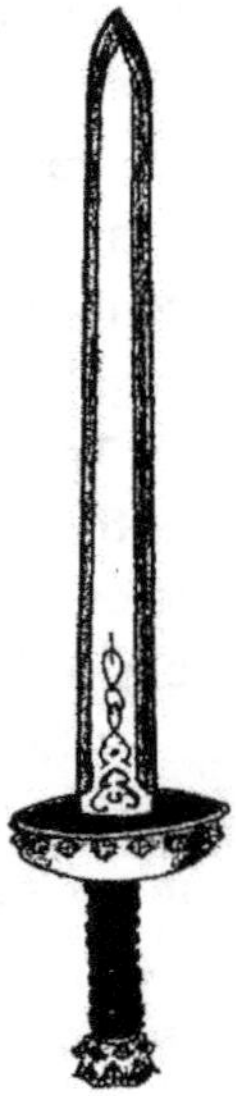

## Sword of Confidence

Any weapon that comes with God's divine body armor is custom-made to fit your hand. If you can hang on to the "sword of confidence" when the flaming arrows are flying and the battle looks lost, you will reap huge rewards.

***So do not throw away your [sword of] confidence; it will be richly rewarded.***

Hebrews 10:35

The "[sword of]" was inserted to picture holding the power of confidence. When you think about it, who wouldn't feel more confident when armed with a sword in their hand, especially one that fights off fear and paralyzing doubts? Some versions of the Bible replace the word "confidence" with courage or boldness, which only sharpens the point.

This same verse appeared in the Leadership Card as a personal reminder of your ability to persevere. Now your Leadership Card can be upgraded to become your first sword of the Spirit. Confidence is not only an important tool to become an authentic leader, but is one of the most valuable swords in your arsenal.

As mentioned before, this biblical principle is about a heavenly reward, but we can apply it to the real world. Warriors would never willingly let go of a real sword during a battle and be defenseless. Yet, how many times have you seen pro athletes get mad and let go of their confidence?

Nevertheless, in any heated situation, never ever let someone rob you of your dignity. As soon as you or your team's confidence is considered dead, the other team is more than happy to put the nail in the coffin. Besides, giving up doesn't win the close games. Fighting to the end while keeping a tenacious grip on your courage and confidence does, and the reward is priceless.

Look again at the story of David and Goliath. God set up several smaller battles to build David's confidence. When all the other warriors ran from Goliath in great fear, David hung on to his confidence despite all the death threats and was "richly rewarded" with Goliath's armor, weapons, and even his head on a stick. These trophies of war would compare with today's version of a Super Bowl ring, the Stanley Cup, or other world championship trophies.

During the game, when the other team is celebrating big plays, don't use your sword of confidence to cut others down. That is not this sword's purpose. A fellow teammate may deserve a kick in the pants but remember, mistakes happen. There will always be times when the best-laid plans go wrong, so don't start hurling word grenades of blame and disgust. In that moment, encourage your teammate to recover his or her lost sword of confidence and use its image as a mental reminder not to give up. Next time they face tough situations, suggest they restore the feeling of wielding a powerful sword by squeezing the ball, golf club, tennis racket, or baseball bat even tighter. If they are empty-handed, have them make a fist and focus on squeezing an invisible sword of confidence as if it were real.

Simple body language will tell you someone's level of confidence. Those with their hands in their pockets are not holding on to God's sword or ready to claim his promise. A reminder of God's reassuring command to be "strong and courageous" (Joshua 1:9) will help them regain unyielding confidence and "be richly rewarded."

The word "sword" appears 365 times in the Bible. Is this a hint to fill your arsenal with a year's supply of inspirational Bible verses and pick a different one for motivation every day? Probably not, because most of these sword verses are about death and military destruction. Only a few meet Paul's definition as a sword of the Spirit and can be used to prepare for competitive situations.

## Most-Talked-About Sword

This sports version of the sword we seek is by far the most popular sword in the Bible. It is talked about 250 times, and it is most recognizable in the story of Samson and Delilah.

> ***The Spirit of the Lord came powerfully upon him so that he tore the lion apart with his bare hands as he might have torn a young goat.***
>
> Judges 14:6

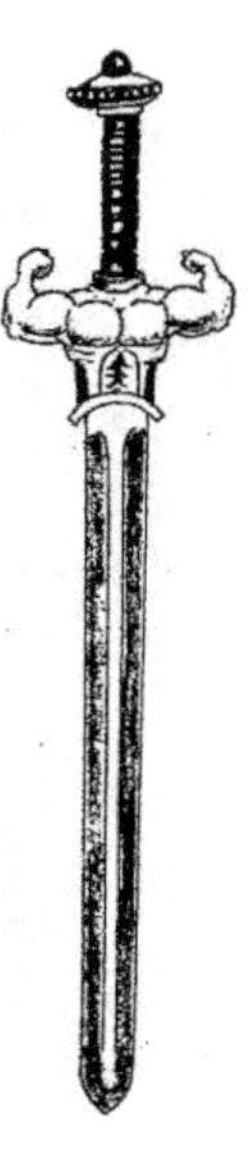

This is a story about Samson, who had crossed paths with a hungry lion and was without a weapon. Fortunately, he received a free download of power from God. Samson was blessed with a "power-sword" that momentarily transformed his normal strength into supernatural arm strength.

If you read the entire story of Samson in Judges 13-16, you will find that he was not a role model. Samson was a gambler. He lost more than his shorts in a bet, which required a second power-sword from God. To pay up, he beat up 30 guys and stole all their clothes. Later, his wife made an ill-advised attempt to tie him up and sell him out to his enemies. After receiving another power-sword, Samson broke free from the heavy ropes. With his anger amplified, he killed 1,000 Philistines with the jawbone of a donkey.

Samson finally revealed the secret of his strength (Judges 16:17) to his wife, Delilah, who then cut his hair while he was sleeping and betrayed him to the Philistines. This time, they took Samson captive. To prevent any escape attempt, the Philistines gouged out his eyes. With all of Samson's character flaws, why would God repeatedly give Samson multiple power-swords, each one increasing in power? Because God used him to achieve a bigger plan, one that caused devastation to the Philistines but a gruesome ending to Samson's life.

Strength and power go together. God, the source of all energy, distributes power as he sees necessary. Notice that in Samson's story, the power needed was delivered directly from the Spirit into Samson's hands. God's power can also be directed by you through prayer. So why not ask God to strengthen your teammates or even yourself?

## Chapter 6

***"I pray that out of his glorious riches he may strengthen you with power through his spirit in your inner being."***

Ephesians 3:16

It would appear that God's spirit is ready to plug into "your inner being" and power-up the entire military base of operations. But if you are feeling a momentary lack of physical energy, the following verse instructs us to take a short break to draw more power.

***But those who wait for Yahweh shall renew their strength; they shall run, and not be weary; they shall walk, and not faint.***

Isaiah 40:31 (WEB)

Jesus had an impressive power-sword that he used frequently to prove his divine connection. He had the power to change water into wine, calm the raging storms, and walk on water. One time when an angry mob was after him, Jesus somehow powered up some type of cloaking device to walk right through the crowd undetected.

Jesus' reputation grew to the point where many people tried to plug into his energy source. In a story in the book of Luke, Jesus talked about the power drain.

***"Who touched me?" Jesus asked. When they all denied it, Peter said, "Master, the people are crowding and pressing against you." But Jesus said, "Someone touched me; I know that power has gone out from me."***

Luke 8:45-46

At that point, a woman went forward and admitted that she had touched his cloak and was instantly healed. She had tapped into his source of energy and depleted a noticeable amount of his power.

When someone is playing a great game, could a pat on the back drain his talent? Or would a high-five of congratulations recharge your power-sword? Forget the silliness. Your game-time hero doesn't have superpowers and according to Google, the human body can only produce 100 watts of energy. Even if you double that amount, your talent might not light up the scoreboard; however, God offers unlimited spiritual energy. Why not plug into the true source of unrestricted power—Jesus?

## Sword of Light

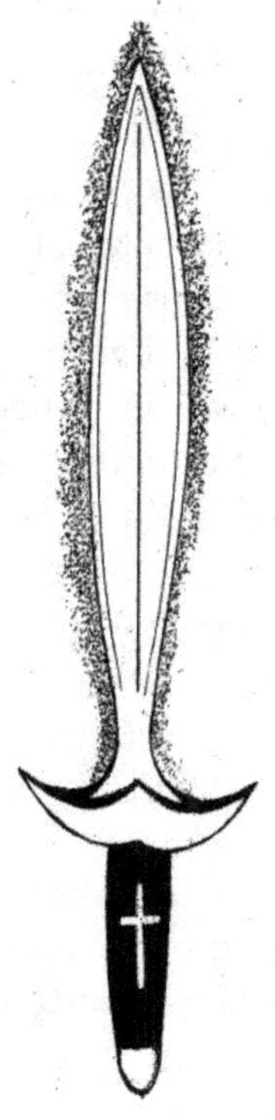

The word "light" in the Bible often symbolizes some of God's attributes and actions. The word "sword" also has its own list of literal and figurative characteristics. If you were to tell your pastor that you have a light-sword that symbolizes a sword of the Spirit, expect a perplexed look as he questions your theology. Combining two words that symbolize many different concepts can be confusing.

Your pastor might be more receptive to your upgraded "sword of the Spirit" if he knew of your *Star Wars* obsession with lightsabers. Now, when wearing your game face, a "light-sword" can represent a favorite "light" verse with the focus on God's power available to light up the universe. By holding on to these verses, you can be the athlete "on fire" who lights up the scoreboard. Let's pursue that sci-fi line of thinking.

In the verse below, Jesus used "light" to describe how your God-given abilities can affect everyone around you. Your mission is not to hide but to blow the lid off and let your talent shine.

> ***"You are the light of the world. A town built on a hill cannot be hidden. Neither do people light a lamp and put it under a bowl. Instead they put it on its stand, and it gives light to everyone in the house. In the same way, let your light shine before others, that they may see your good deeds and glorify your Father in heaven."***
>
> Matthew 5:14-16

People who stand out in a group have a unique energy. Some would call this charisma or charm. It's as if their mental warehouse has glowing neon signs that attract everyone around them to see what's going on. In this passage, Jesus asserts that when it comes to influencing others, behavior is very powerful. Setting a good example by completing "good deeds" is just as important as what you believe. Consider your light-sword to be a spiritual weapon that makes your personality shine brighter and stand out. When others notice your newfound glow of confidence, share the source of your energy with them.

## Light It Up, Up, Up!

Great athletes can light up the scoreboard. In football, basketball, hockey, and soccer, it's important to create scoring opportunities. Certain athletes always find a way to get open before receiving the ball or puck. It is a skill that requires awareness to make the right decisions that will put you on the right path to score points. The following two promises symbolize light-swords you might want to add to your arsenal:

***What you decide on will be done, and light will shine on your ways.***
Job 22:28

***Your word is a lamp for my feet, a light on my path.***
Psalm 119:105

Just imagine getting together with teammates to relive the glory days, to share that common bond by talking about the great plays and the tough wins, and even reminiscing about the abusive crowd noise when playing at the opponents' home field or court.

Over 2,000 years ago, the followers of Jesus shared a traumatic bonding experience that parallels a modern-day sporting event.

***Remember those earlier days after you had received the [sword of] light, when you endured in a great conflict full of suffering. Sometimes you were publicly exposed to insult and persecution; at other times you stood side by side with those who were so treated.***
Hebrews 10:32-33

The followers of Jesus endured tough spiritual battles, even death threats and beatings, but they persevered, empowered by a sword of the Spirit.

Here is another light-sword verse that you may want to add to your arsenal.

## Chapter 6

***The night is nearly over; the day is almost here. So let us put aside the deeds of darkness and put on the armor of light.***

Romans 13:12

# Triple-Edged Sword

Some athletes have to do it bigger and better than anyone else. This sword should satisfy that mindset. Its three blades are similar to what you find on the end of a hunting arrow. It combines a triple threat of the most important qualities needed to play with the heart of a warrior.

***For the Spirit God gave us does not make us timid, but gives us power, love and self-discipline.***

2 Timothy 1:7

Your job is to protect the kingdom, and this is the heavenly recipe to create self-confidence. God's Spirit is making a "soul" connection to give you an enhanced power sword that unifies your other two entities. The mind ends up with extra self-discipline and your heart accepts an attitude that would "love" to take care of business.

When you break-down this verse, self-discipline is needed to streamline your mental game. That means accomplishing your short term-long term goals in a systematic way and ignoring the emotional impulses to take shortcuts that come back to bite you.

What about a spirit of love? That's the heart's area of expertise. The type of love we are looking for is found in the passages of 1 Corinthians 13. Only now, the focus is on a soldier's love that always perseveres, protects, and never fails.

Maybe you are content with your timid spirit, but timidity and hesitation are not in God's sports vocabulary or even his playbook. When this combination of power, love, and self-discipline are forged together to build confidence in your heart, mind, and soul, great things will happen. Now that you have a triple-edged sword to improve your performance by weaponizing your mental game, are you going to use it?

## Hidden Instruction Manual

The search to find the best swords of the Spirit and to use them properly will require spiritual wisdom. Wisdom can be weaponized to act as a word grenade. Just pull the pin and it quietly blows up the confusion standing in your way. Now you can clarify what you need to best unify the head and the heart. Thankfully, God doesn't judge us on our limited and sometimes foolish understanding of his plan or the lack of courage to use his weapons. In the following promise, he never hesitates to hand out instructional wisdom.

***If any of you lacks wisdom, you should ask God, who gives generously to all without finding fault, and it will be given to you.***

James 1:5

Your prayer request for warrior insight can be as simple as asking, "What is the wise thing to do?" In other words, you are asking for a game plan to help the head and heart deal with reality. Just don't expect the answer to always pop into your head. God can send it FedEx from anywhere in the world. If you are looking for same-day delivery, the wisdom you seek may show up in the Bible in front of you. Or you may have to wait for a Sunday delivery from the sermon at church.

Since you can call on God's promise to distribute wisdom as many times as you wish, what is your excuse for *not* asking for divine wisdom? God is generous. He will not fault you or your bad attitude for doing it the hard way, or when your simple request repeats like a broken record. God will always honor your intent to seek him. Do not doubt his power to deliver.

Opening God's powerful arsenal can be a game-changer. In the Ephesians passage on wearing God's armor, the text is in the present tense. It can be read as a whispering suggestion to "Take the sword" or read as if God is the head coach, commanding his athletes to "TAKE THE SWORD, TAKE THE SWORD!" Can it be any clearer that the sword of the Spirit is designed to help you weaponize your thoughts to bring out the inner warrior? Even if you're on the bench, be prepared, don't go into the game without a sword to protect God's kingdom.

The sword is God's word. Make it yours, keep it alive, and use it with a purpose. Fill your arsenal with God's written weapons to help you play with honor and to silence any fear, doubt, and anxiety. Don't wait until the outcome of the game is on the line before deciding to pick out a biblical weapon to weaponize your thoughts. When great athletes wear the face of a warrior, they don't procrastinate or even hesitate, they have the ammo to anticipate. So, before the game starts, be proactive, arm yourself, and become the best at what you were meant to be!

The armor of God can also change the entire team dynamic. Instead of worrying about who is going to screw up and let the team down, the focus is on who's playing the best and what sword they are packing. When a few teammates achieve greatness, it is contagious. The competitive attitude kicks in, and others will suit up to achieve a higher level of excellence.

## Choose Your Weapon!

Now that God's sports arsenal has been exposed, the hunt is on to find the best weapons that work for you. To encourage you to take that first step, we have revealed three weapons of emotion, identified four of the hidden swords of the Spirit, numerous word grenades, and discovered that the military base of operations is equipped with sophisticated hunting technology.

Are you still going through that boot camp experience and requiring more weapons of confidence? The Bible has 35 more verses on the subject. Are you interested in all types of biblical weaponry? As mentioned, you will find at least 365 sword verses and numerous others about weapons other than swords. There are more than 400 verses about gaining more power and strength and more passages on seeking the wisdom to make it all work.

What are you waiting for? As you can see, the Bible contains a lifetime supply of information on battle strategies and weapons. Every area of your mental game can improve if you will tap into the unlimited power revealed in God's word. Just find weapons that make your inner warrior come to life. Your best swords of the Spirit should be sharp enough to hack to pieces any negative paralysis and surgically remove any defeatist attitude of the heart.

> ***For the word of God is alive and active. Sharper than any double-edged sword, it penetrates even to dividing soul and spirit, joints and marrow; it judges the thought and attitudes of the heart.***
>
> Hebrews 4:12

Hopefully, your sports perception of the Bible has changed. Many people think of the Bible as an old-fashioned book filled with religious stuff that only churchy people can understand. Where is the motivation for an athlete to rely on a book like that or think it has anything of value for the sports mind? As we have discovered, the Bible is God's arsenal, and we are commanded to select a sword of the Spirit to take with us every day. The strength of your opponent and the complexity of the battle will determine which verses you choose.

On top of that, God's greatest commandment is about a relationship that brings all three of your entities to the table, including your military base of operations. By bringing it all into a loving relationship with God, you will experience an epic level of encouragement and direction. During your sports journey, God will empower you with a love that accomplishes great things and lets others "see your good deeds and glorify your Father in heaven" (Matthew 5:16).

# Extreme Mental Games

## Chapter 7

Even after Chicago Bulls superstar Michael Jordan retired, some experts still considered him not only the best athlete in the NBA but the best athlete on the planet! Experts who sing the praises of LeBron tend to forget about Michael's six championship rings, five MVP awards, and 10 NBA scoring titles. While it is true that the Boston Celtics have more players with more championship rings, it is how Michael earned his trophies that makes him stand above the others. During the playoffs, Michael's numbers would always improve as he stepped up as the team's leader. His talent shifted into overdrive when the game was on the line or when the opportunity to take the game-winning shot presented itself.

Before games, what type of mental preparation did Michael Jordan do to improve his greatness? Did he study a complicated 60-page game plan while guzzling Gatorade, the sports drink he wholeheartedly endorsed? No, not even close, but Michael's preparation did have an extremely superstitious aspect. There's a significant story behind his jersey number 23, and his pre-game ritual included eating a 23-ounce steak four hours before the game. In addition, Michael wore his powder-blue University of North Carolina game shorts under his Chicago Bulls uniform. In order to hide his college shorts, Michael wore long, baggy shorts, a fashion statement that spelled the demise of the short shorts in men's basketball.

We might expect Michael and LeBron to prepare their most powerful weapons in similar ways since both have achieved scoring greatness. LeBron is known for spending a great deal of time on mental preparation for the next game, but Michael has more scoring titles, so you would expect to hear Michael talk about his offensive deep thinking as well. That is not the case. In his book *For the Love of the Game,* Michael admits, "I didn't practice Zen or sit in a room and meditate."

Before the pre-game distractions started, Michael's competitive heart would not let him sit still. It drove him to get on the court as early as possible. The basketball court is where he satisfied the needs of his analytical mind. He would visualize his goals while using his shoot-around time to enhance what he wanted to accomplish and polish his jump shot with 150 free throws. It appears he was building a balanced inventory to satisfy the needs of both his heart and his mind. Once the sports warehouse was filled to capacity, Michael's command center was ready to execute his signature scoring moves at game time.

Filling the sports warehouse with upcoming scoring scenarios makes sense, but why did Michael shoot so many free throws? No team would consider fouling Michael Jordan 150 times. Some athletes would see this as a dreaded punishment, not as needed mental preparedness. Why spend so much time practicing an exercise from a grade-school P.E. class? Shouldn't half a dozen free throws be enough to give him the big picture?

Michael was not alone when it comes to extreme repetition. Kobe Bryant, who retired after a 20-year career with the Los Angeles Lakers, liked the feel of a real basketball in his hands. Practicing game situations in a virtual reality was not enough. After Kobe won his first championship ring, he changed his off-season routine. In Phil Jackson's book *Eleven Rings,* Kobe revealed his program of taking 2,000 shots a day. Even if his daily total were rounded up to impress his coach—say he only took 1,500 shots a day—it would still be an amazing workout.

Kobe was then motivated to start the season with an energetic new confidence and a spectacular display of talent. Fans went wild over Kobe's new moves. He was unstoppable and led the league with a near-50% shooting percentage against the best defenders in the world.

Sadly, the Los Angeles Lakers legend Kobe Bryant was killed in a helicopter crash in California. At 41 years old, along with his 13-year-old daughter, their lives ended much too soon.

The NFL did a study of running backs in the 1980s and found an unusual group of athletes. When these backs carried the football 10 or more times per game, their average yards per carry *increased* as the game went on. The more times they touched the ball, the better they played. Instead of getting tired in the fourth quarter, they became more energized. Analysts concluded that these athletes needed a certain number of reps to get into the flow of the game.

## Recording Muscle Control

To explain the need for excessive sports repetition, let's turn to information technology. Today, many devices are available to store information. If 100 people were surveyed and asked to pick a digital device that could record and replay their thoughts and mental images, a DVD player would be one of the top five answers. Although it's considered old technology, you can still keep a library of DVDs. That makes it easy to apply the biblical concept to "store up" and bring out the "good things." Michael's pre-game mental activity can be compared to a DVD player/recorder, one that records every shot he takes and warehouses it for the upcoming game.

The normal DVD player/burner records the typical visual and audio formats. The one in the human mind is designed to record more detailed information than just the five senses. Before and during a game, your brain never stops recording as it creates endless stacks of DVDs, many with irrelevant details. This becomes a problem when you're trying to find the game information you need. Time spent digging through stacks of worthless DVDs slows down your reaction time. Michael, however, found a way to take advantage of the non-stop recording process. He filled up his mental warehouse by recording the physical act of shooting, leaving no room for distractions.

In Michael's case, his pre-game program involved recording a simple task multiple times to prepare for taking big shots in big games. His internal DVD burner needed to fill the sports warehouse with 150 free throws before he could roll out his scoring machine and begin his assault on the defense. His stack of DVDs included not only a visual recording of what he planned to do, but what he needed to put the ball through the hoop—*muscle control*. He was using his *body* instead of his *brain* to create a neuromuscular connection.

Perhaps you have heard of muscle memory. Muscle memory and muscle control are similar. Shooting free throws involves muscle memory because the distance is always the same, and the muscle movement needed to sink the shot is repetitive. Perfecting a touchdown dance routine also requires muscle memory. Muscle control, on the other hand, is what allows you to adapt to the situation and shoot from any distance during the game.

Nike's iconic "Just do it" slogan has been a major part of an extraordinarily successful ad campaign for years. It helped sell as many athletic shoes as McDonald's has burgers. It could be the battle cry for all athletes who prepare like Michael Jordan. Their secret of staying in the zone requires using more muscle than brainpower. That process of just doing "it" and then recording "it" on a DVD provides the type of payload for a superior performance.

**Fuel loaded for launch. Begin countdown!**

Some athletes don't realize they need extreme repetition. Since they don't have a pre-game program, they attempt to organize what needs to be executed during the game. You have seen this happen numerous times but may not have recognized it. The next time you see a running back pound the ground with his fist, or a receiver hit his helmet with both hands after making a mental mistake, he may have just burned a new DVD with new internal directives. It now contains the muscle control commands to hang on to the ball or zig when he should have zagged after seeing an open road to the end zone.

What is muscle control? The simplest way to understand it is to look at the lack of it. Have you ever tried to write a sentence or sign your name by using your other hand? How about throwing a football or baseball with your non-dominant arm? The real problem is not the size of your muscles but the lack of neuromuscular connections to make your muscles work properly.

Think of muscle control as a software program that controls the physical part of your body. Multiple software apps are running right now. We don't notice them because they are running on a subconscious level, but to read this page, detailed instructions are controlling your eye muscles to move from word to word. Think about the muscle control required to keep your head balanced on top of your neck. Your head is about the size and weight of a bowling ball, so a software app is triggering muscles to push or pull to keep it from needlessly flopping and bobbing around. To walk, the necessary app must be running to synchronize your joints to work properly so you don't fall over like a drunken sailor.

To compete in sports, your brain's high-speed software must deal with a slow physical connection. Your large individual joints have a limited maximum speed. Try pitching a fastball by locking your shoulder and using only your elbow motion. If you are lucky, the floating ball might make it to home plate. How can a pitcher throw a 90+ mph fastball? He has pre-recorded the detailed instructions that associate a fastball with the muscle control needed for speed and accuracy. Once he selects the right software app to play, his muscles fire at just the right time to synchronize and amplify the forward movement created by every joint in his body. This forward motion from his toes to his fingertips is perfectly timed to reach maximum speed before launching the ball toward the catcher's mitt.

## Extreme Positive Visualization

Mike Singletary played middle linebacker for the Chicago Bears from 1981 to 1992. Before being voted to the Pro Bowl 10 times, before leading the team in tackles year after year, and even before earning a Super Bowl ring, as a college player Mike was told he was "too short, too slow, and too small to play middle linebacker in the NFL." That type of trash-talk would have a devastating effect in every building on the military base of operations.

But this echoing fear didn't stop Mike from realizing his NFL dreams. Instead, he developed a strong mental preparation program that more than compensated for his alleged weaknesses. He improved his game-time performance by doing extra homework. He would not only study the coach's list of key plays but claimed to have memorized the opposing team's entire playbook. Mentally, there is a big difference between being familiar with a play and seeing it play out in the theater in your mind. His thinking was, "They can't run anything I haven't seen before." This technique enabled Mike to gain that extra step needed to lead the team in tackles per game. The visual imagery he used to memorize plays fired-up the motor neurons needed to chase down and tackle anyone carrying the ball.

Mike Singletary and Michael Jordan are two great athletes who played at the top of their respective sports. They consistently achieved greatness with totally different pre-game preparation, yet they had one thing in common—repetition. Michael needed more physical repetition on a real basketball court, and Mike required extreme repetition performed in his mind. Even though they had their own personal style to fill the sports warehouse with relentless intensity, both men achieved maximum results.

## Extreme Aggressiveness

My high school classmate Chucky was a big strong farm boy who was a quiet nerd at heart. He always came to school wearing his classic pocket protector to shield his shirt from leaky pens and wore small round Harry Potter glasses. Resembling a 1970s version of the Steve Urkel character (without the annoying voice), he was a friendly, happy-go-lucky guy who smiled a lot. His classmates discovered, however, that if you teased the big farm boy, he had two faces.

They would start by verbally tormenting him, which did not seem to bother him. But when he was physically pushed back on his heels, an aggressive passion would begin to grow in Chuck's eyes. When his heart could take no more, the seemingly ineffective word grenades they kept tossing would simultaneously detonate. Once that explosion took place, Chucky quickly transformed into the ultimate angry warrior, and everyone yelled, "Get out of here! Run for your lives!" Fortunately, he did not run very fast because he was big enough and strong enough to pound anyone into the ground like a fence post.

Bullying is not acceptable. But when the loudmouth media starts spitting verbal venom or the opposing team hits you with trash-talk, it can definitely jump-start an aggressive attitude. Most athletes aren't born with a bad attitude, so they need more than just talk to load some aggressive firepower. They need to have someone show them a total lack of respect by pushing them around. When backed into a corner, their blood will start to boil and drive them to play their best.

Before scrimmages and games, I would have the micro-soccer players do some shoulder pushing. The main reason was so they would not fall down every time they bumped into another player. But it also worked to get their little hearts pumping with enough aggressiveness to replace any pre-game jitters.

If your coach doesn't have any Chucky drills to deal with aggressiveness, develop your own. Start with a pushing-and- shoving contest to begin the transformation. Add some trash-talk that targets what matters most. Keep your personal coaching instructions real and positive. Get each other fired up until you start to feel that aggressive attitude followed by an aggressive sweat. The big guns of aggressiveness are now loaded and will come out blazing at game time.

## Extreme Sports Tattoos

Jerry Rice was the son of a bricklayer, so his summer jobs included physical labor and moving tons of bricks. During an interview he said, "I have such strong hands that if the ball is even close, I'll catch it." Jerry was implying that even in the NFL passes are rarely perfect. He was prepared to increase his catch radius by calculating the point of impact.

When this targeting tool is switched on, expect a crowd-pleasing performance. Nothing is more thrilling than seeing a pro receiver change directions in mid-air, make an unbelievable one-handed catch, and then land with both feet inbounds.

The technical term for mentally measuring distances is called "depth perception." Besides sports, driving a car is the most common activity that enables this part of your brain. Red brake lights are supposed to remind you to switch on this mental tool and avoid a fender bender. Even then, the number of rear-end collisions was so high that a third brake light emerged as a better reminder.

In sports, why crash and burn when you can avoid an embarrassing mental breakdown such as an air ball, a golf shot in the lake, or a sloppy tackle? You cannot attach a red flashing light to the backboard, golf green, or running back, but you can use a sports tattoo to turn on this targeting tool. Simply signing your name on the ball will not have enough fundamental instructions to do the job. Being prepared for any game situation takes an extreme sports tattoo.

## Establishing a Target Lock

If you were to shoot your best friend between the eyes with a squirt gun, you would notice that your dominant eye is doing all the aiming. Closing the other eye does not change where the gun is aimed. But, when your dominant eye is closed, it appears the gun has moved. This is because two separate perspectives enter the brain. When your depth perception is switched on, your brain is receiving binocular clues. Each eye is seeing different pictures that contain the clues needed to calculate distance. These calculations are typically accurate up to 20 feet away from the target, which is just beyond the high school 3-point line. Beyond 30 feet, our eyes assess the size of the target to determine its distance. The smaller the flag appears on the green, the greater the distance.

To play fast-moving sports, this depth perception assessment must occur at high speed. In baseball, it's important to have this mental tool ready before entering the batter's box. When facing a 90+ mph fastball, it takes less than .5 seconds to reach home plate (Answers.com). Any chance of hitting the ball during that brief moment requires calculating the point of impact in the strike zone and using the right motor neurons to connect a moving bat to hit the ball. The following sports tattoo will turn on your laser focus and prepare you to react at game speed.

**Chapter 7**

# Engaging Target Lock

## *Ready, Aim, Fire!*

If you are into combat video games this image is all you need to know. Your brain is already wired to support a live version of a video game targeting tool. Next time you walk on the field, visualize this targeting tattoo on whatever you are trying to hit, catch or throw, and pull the trigger to get the job done. To be consistent in sports, however, your personal gunsights require specialized upgrades to incorporate a number of self-coaching instructions.

The four matchsticks are a reminder to switch on the "matching" process to calculate the point of impact and process visual information *at least* four times faster than normal. In a football situation, the switch to game speed changes a receiver's perspective. It slows down the game situation so he can anticipate the football's trajectory and adjust his catch radius.

The padlock is a reminder to stay locked like a laser beam on whatever your target may be, no matter what distraction might try to stop you. Even if catching a pass means a mid-air collision with two linebackers, you will stay focused on the prize and not drop the ball.

The image of a chain allows you to modify your muscle-control app to fit a variety of game situations. To apply this concept when playing defense in man-to-man coverage, place this targeting tattoo on your competitor and keep him on a short chain. On offense, a receiver would target the ball and attach the chain to his dominant hand. When thus "chained" to the football, the entire body works together to make the catch. Even when a deflected pass can cause you to jump up or dive to the turf, the ball can still end up in your hands.

## Multiple Bogeys

A receiver has only one target—the ball. On the other end of the pass, it's a lot more complicated. Before completing a Ready-Aim-Fire sequence, the quarterback must first locate the receiver in his gun sights. When multiple targets are spread across an entire football field, time is a limiting factor. Tagging all potential receivers and anticipating their routes will speed up the search for that go-to receiver. Now you know why Joe Montana walked up to the line of scrimmage with a blank look on his face.

When a quarterback tags multiple targets, his peripheral vision automatically sweeps back and forth like a radar antenna as he searches for a wide-open receiver. Once a target-lock is found, he zooms in as if using military-grade binoculars. He then makes the necessary calculations to throw a catchable ball.

That takes care of the "Ready-Aim" part. To "Fire," a quarterback must execute the proper muscle-control app. Highly skilled quarterbacks add an extra step to determine the defensive threat. A common quarterback failure is not recognizing two defenders inside the targeting area. When a quarterback ignores a double team, he is often locked in on one receiver and fails to check off that receiver and find a better target.

*Go defense!* Maybe your job is to keep the quarterback in your gun sights. The targeting concept is basically the same, just make sure the football is your primary target. Before putting the quarterback in the crosshairs, place a laser-target lock on the ball and then brand it with a favorite possessive tattoo. Zoom out to see the entire athlete and be sure to target anyone else who might advance the ball. That way, you can switch to a new target without hesitation.

## Bonus Features

This target-lock tattoo automatically sends you into "combat mode" and activates your radar tracking equipment along with the other apps needed to outsmart your adversary. Now, trick plays won't fake you out. You will be able to evaluate subtle clues from the quarterback's eyes and body language that betray his intentions and never lose track of the ball. This ability to read the play is similar to identifying a wild animal at an African game preserve. You only need to see a part of an ear or trunk to recognize the lion or elephant in the tall grass. It is a simple matching process, so don't sweat the details and let the processing power at Strategic Command do the work.

## Target Lock Confirmed

## Locked & Loaded to Take Down the Quarterback

In many sports, the need to keep a laser-lock on a target is a two-step process. Before making that chip shot onto the green, a golfer will target the flag and then put his or her head down to target the ball. In soccer, tennis, and baseball, athletes will aim at the open spot first before targeting the ball. Your ability to adapt this targeting tattoo to various game situations will improve its accuracy and your performance.

## Extreme Ball Security

Now let's work on a sports tattoo that will simplify the task of ball control and avoid the most devastating mental breakdown in every game: *turnovers*.

To catch a ball in any sport takes focused concentration on the ball with some degree of focus on your hands. When your hands catch a ball, a muscle-control app is also needed to cushion it, commonly referred to in football as having "soft hands." Without it, the ball is dropped or deflected off muscle-bound fingers. Once the impact has been absorbed, the receiver must grip the ball to complete the catch.

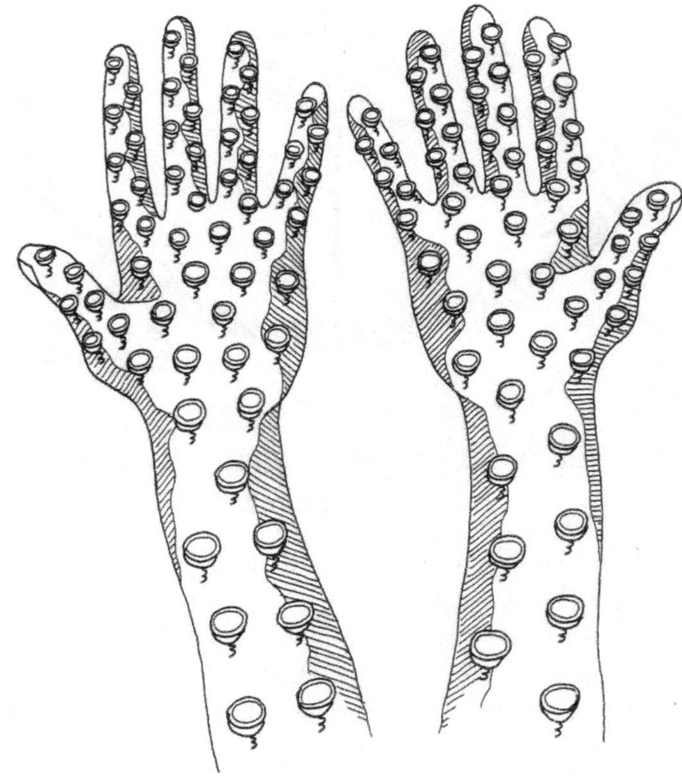

**Sticky Fingers**

This illustration symbolizes a focus on your hands and the need to maintain ball security. The design features small springs under the suction cups to represent the muscle-control app needed to cushion the impact of the ball ("soft hands"). The small suction cups are a reminder to grip the ball with the tenacity of an octopus. Notice the higher density of suction cups on the hands than on the arms. It's always better to use your hands for ball control, especially when making a one-handed catch.

A good sports tattoo like this will require extreme emotion to activate a stellar performance. It already contains enough logic to captivate the analytical mind, so to satisfy the heart, attach one of your favorite aggressive, possessive phrases to both your hands and the ball. Just as the word "Squirrel!" triggered the sleepy old dog to alter his behavior, your customized command will create an unbreakable bond with the ball.

In an attempt to steal the ball, a defender can use a sports tattoo to create turnovers. There is a brief window of opportunity when a quarterback or ball carrier thinks he is under the protection of the linemen and shifts his laser focus downfield. In that instant just before he is blind-sided there is minimal ball security. That is also true when he receives a face-to-face *stop-'em-cold* hit. The impact activates the need for self-preservation. The head and heart are momentarily distracted as they evaluate the bone-crunching experience, leaving the ball with minimum protection. To take advantage of these turnover opportunities, you need to have a specialized sports tattoo in place. Let's organize your skills to strip the ball from your opponent's hands.

## Chapter 7

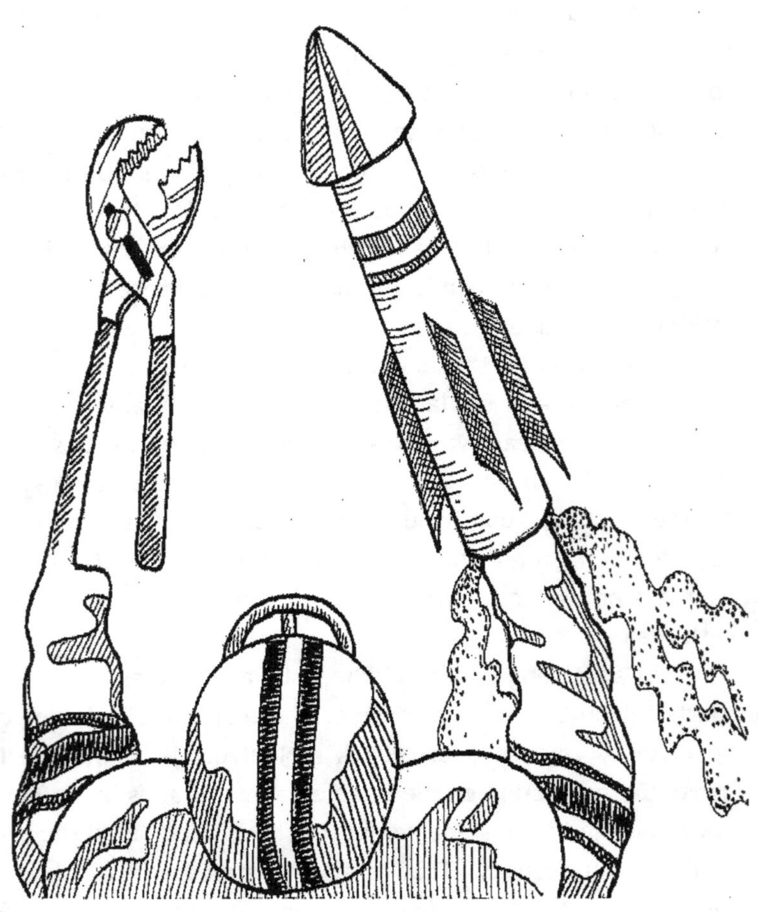

## Make the Hit, Steal the Ball, and Run!

One of the dangers of attempting to strip the ball is focusing only on the ball and allowing the ball carrier to break free and gain extra yards. To deal with the problem and make sure there is no escape, we added power pinchers to the image above. Sometimes the play moves so quickly that the defender can barely get a hand on the ball carrier. This sports tattoo helps you hang on to his jersey with vise-grip power until reinforcements arrive.

Whoever controls the football controls the game. The football is the high-value target, the *hot property* everybody wants, so we use a heat-seeking missile to symbolize targeting the ball's likely location. Since the ball may not be visible, knowing your adversary's ball-carrying tendencies can help your built-in radar system track the unseen target. You can also use the ball carrier's elbow to anticipate the ball's location. You can trigger this tattoo with one of your favorite possessive phrases such as "That ball is mine!" When the rocket smoke builds, muscle power is now rerouted to blast it free. After you have experimented with this exercise, mentally tattoo these images on your hands to activate your newfound ball-snatching skills.

## To Breathe or Not to Breathe? That is the Question

When you break it down, you find that several mental activities can limit your ability to concentrate and even neutralize your power when in beast mode. Breathing is one of them. Every cell in your body needs oxygen to survive, and the need increases with physical activity. It takes mental concentration to monitor and maintain the proper oxygen levels in your bloodstream. If your oxygen level falls too low, brain damage and death can result. If it rises too high, you can hyperventilate and become dizzy.

Out-of-control competitive passion can also limit your ability to focus on a simple task at hand. Just watch as the camera zooms in on the contestants participating in a reality TV show. As they await the final decision as to who goes home, fearful emotion takes over. It becomes so overwhelming that it even paralyzes the ability to breathe. To keep from collapsing, the contestants will manually take a deep breath and blow it out slowly to calm their nerves.

## Chapter 7

When sports mental connections are added into the mix, it is even harder to multi-task and stay focused. To maintain consistency, many top athletes control their breathing and pause while executing complex mental calculations. In professional women's tennis, that breathless process ends with a very un-ladylike grunt when returning the volley. In the weight room, the grunts and groans to become the alpha-male are very noticeable (and even exaggerated whenever a lady is present).

Anytime you cut off someone's air supply, you have their undivided attention. When full concentration is needed to avoid being tackled, running backs will postpone the distraction of breathing until the play ends and then return to the huddle huffing and puffing.

The key to executing complex mental connections is to organize your breathing beforehand. A brief pause after inhaling will allow you to attach a sports tag to an opposing team jersey or to burn a permanent tattoo on the ball. If you can just hold your breath long enough to imagine the smoke rising from branding the leather ball with a targeting image, then you know it's a sweet tattoo.

To take down a quarterback on the run may require several deep breaths before the play starts. Take in enough oxygen to allow you to execute a target lock and hit the turbo-boost button without running out of gas.

Having trouble shooting free throws? Zoom in and place your targeting tattoo on the edge of the rim. Hold off on breathing just long enough to light it up with a circle of flames. Now visualize the ball going through the flames and into the basket with nothing but net. Or, before the ref hands you the ball, select a muscle-control app by physically going through the motion of shooting an invisible basketball. Reaching a high level of mental concentration will improve your confidence when the game is on the line.

## Universal Sports Tattoos

Several of these mental tattoos focus on the skills needed to be a wide receiver, a position known for its high failure rate. But these tattoos can be adapted to almost any sport or position that requires you to calculate the point of impact and maintain ball control. Creating a game-changing tattoo is easy, just make sure its fundamental design makes sense for you. When you mix in some weaponized emotions, you will improve your combat skills and game-time performance.

If you want to add your new sports tattoos to your collection of body ink, think twice. Before making any of these images permanent, test your own images by tattooing them on a pair of sports gloves or a T-shirt. Your creativity is a key to success, and you may want to make improvements each time you step on the field.

Seek new ideas from teammates to improve your own sports tattoos. Track and test their designs to upgrade your skills when in combat mode. Having the best weapons in your arsenal can lead to performances that move you up the depth chart. Soon, you can experience the thrill of making a game-winning catch or a 3-point buzzer-beater. Getting high-fives from teammates feels better than getting the evil eye when you whiff on a game-winning opportunity.

# Disarming Performance Anxiety

## Chapter 8

John Madden, Super Bowl-winning head coach and former NFL analyst on *Monday Night Football*, would frequently recall stories from his coaching days with the Oakland Raiders. One story was about a player whose pre-game program delayed his team's taking the field. Before each game, this player would remodel his sports warehouse with walls of fear. Those walls would start to close in and make him feel trapped in his own mind and in the locker room. The only way out was by hosting a vomiting meet-and-greet with the locker room toilet.

Once his ritual of throwing up was finished, the team was ready to play! Game after game, the team waited patiently as this player fought a losing battle with the toughest competitor that an athlete will ever face: *the fear of impending doom!*

What formidable opponent or situation did this player weaponize with fear to create such future disasters? Who or whatever it was must be disarmed, because his pre-game performance in front of the toilet will not inspire an invincible warrior's vibe among teammates. This athlete was clueless when it came to keeping a laser focus on what's important—winning. Your pre-game program is about surrounding yourself with God's weapons and making plans for victory—not replaying failures and feeling defeated. Sadly, the process of weaponizing your thoughts to become a *worrier* is identical to the process of becoming a *warrior*, and the effort required is about the same. Someday, this athlete will look back at his untapped potential and regret not becoming so much more.

## Chapter 8

Phil Jackson, former head coach of both the Chicago Bulls and the L.A. Lakers, knew a thing or two about performance anxiety. After winning six NBA championships with the Bulls and five more with the Lakers, Phil has been inside the heads of many struggling athletes. When it comes to the question of why athletes lose their lunch, the best guess could be taken from the list of fears Phil describes in his latest book *Eleven Rings: The Soul of Success*. These are some of the harsh realities of life that young men face in the NBA.

> ***Most players live in a state of constant anxiety, worrying about whether they're going to be hurt or humiliated, cut or traded, or, worst of all, make a foolish mistake that will haunt them for the rest of their lives.***
>
> **Phil Jackson**

The world of sports is a dangerous place both physically and mentally. Anxiety retention could easily shut down every part of the military base with paralyzing negativity. You would no longer have access to your command center, sports warehouse, or even the armory. It is only natural that nobody wants to be caught making a game-changing mistake that lets the team down. Further, sports highlight films and blooper reels reinforce the pressure to play a perfect game. But mistakes happen. Jerry Rice has dropped touchdown passes; Tiger Woods has missed tournament-winning putts, and Kobe Bryant has missed last-second game-winning shots numerous times.

Most athletes, both pro and amateur, have struggled with some type of performance anxiety. It was surprising that a superstar such as Jerry Rice would admit to getting a little nervous before games. His pre-game anxiety was created by the fear of dropping the ball and letting down his dad or his teammates. In most post-game locker room interviews, pro athletes want to convince their fans that they have nerves of steel and unshakable confidence. They do this, of course, as they are getting dressed and putting on their deodorant. No one wants to admit to having pre-game jitters or creating a nervous sweat, but the giant deodorant companies bank on knowing better!

Let's circle back to chapter 3, where we discussed the military base of operations. Our mission was to take control of the sports warehouse by doing some drama replacement therapy. We changed your attitude towards the most hated practice drills. Next, we moved on to filling your arsenal with weapons of emotion and powerful ammo by using sports tags and sports tattoos. All this upgraded firepower should have annihilated your game-day worries. If not, you may be dealing with old war wounds caused by the shrapnel from explosive mistakes.

Time is supposed to heal old wounds, but that is not always the case. When the clock is counting down before kickoff, you may be stuck in the past with a hidden inventory of insecurities. Once a renewed fear takes control, it's tough to see a confident future. A familiar last-minute game plan is to stuff down any negativity and put on a tough guy "game face." Pretending the conflict doesn't exist by trying to "Fake it until you make it!" won't stop the old subliminal inventory from eating you up inside. This attempted quick fix continually fails, so call a "time-out!" Throw out the old game plan and go with God's program. God doesn't want you to feel overwhelmed and paralyzed by what is going on inside your sports warehouse. Your energy should be focused on his game plan and not dealing with a cold sweat in front of the toilet.

We found God's basic principles for mental preparation in chapter 2. It required storing up the "good things" to produce the "good fruit." When John Madden's athlete exploded from storing up too much internal anxiety, the overflow was flushed down the locker room toilet. Did this process eliminate all the heart-pounding anxiety he was retaining? Probably not, but it can provide some temporary relief by freeing up space in the sports warehouse; however, the bulk of his original fears and failures were left intact.

The common remedy for avoiding anxiety retention is to be better organized. That's true; it helps to reduce stress, but the space in your mental warehouse is limited. There are plenty of organizational programs to help you squeeze more "good things" into your day, but what about unloading the shelves full of bad inventory? The experience of past failures can be disastrous and produce negative paralysis, so the big question is this: How do you eliminate all the "bad fruit" without losing your entire lunch? The writer of Hebrews used a sports analogy to help solve the problem.

> ***Therefore, since we are surrounded by such a great cloud of witnesses, let us throw off everything that hinders and the sin that so easily entangles. And let us run with perseverance the race marked out for us.***
>
> Hebrews 12:1

Does this make sense? You have gotten yourself tangled up with faulty expectations based on past experience and those thoughts are holding you back—so deal with the disasters in your life. Cut yourself loose, break free, and leave the wreckage behind. The following verse tells us how anxiety also affects the performance of your most powerful entity.

> ***Anxiety weighs down the heart, but a kind word cheers it up.***
>
> Proverbs 12:25

The heart is the happiest when harmony is maintained by having all things work together for good. Then there are times of conflict and anxiousness. The word "anxiety" in the Bible can be defined as *being pulled in different directions*. The battle to do the right thing (remain sinless) instead of taking a shortcut that ends in regrets is ever-present. In most cases, however, the feeling of anxiety or panic arises from daunting deadlines, not being in the right place at the right time, or being overwhelmed by not meeting high expectations as a stressful event approaches.

Have you ever talked to someone who can't seem to lose the negativity and appears to be carrying the weight of the world on their shoulders? It looks like they are about to blow up or on the verge of becoming burned out. Yet, when you understand the mechanics of what is going on, it doesn't take much for you to lighten their load and turn the heart around. Thoughtful words can be used to "encourage one another and build each other up" (1 Thessalonians 5:11). Positive affirmations can help someone cast away their cares and change their entire day.

A present-day metaphor of this anxious-heart healing scripture could be "No wonder you're exhausted; you are carrying a backpack full of anxiety." Hauling around mental baggage can feel just as heavy as real baggage, so maybe it's time to deal with that invisible backpack. Empty it or somehow cut yourself free by removing the straps. Adopting a process of letting go can be therapeutic for your head as well as your heart.

In the last chapter, you were asked to transfer your thoughts and images onto a familiar medium, DVDs. If an athlete were to carry a backpack (or a sports warehouse) full of DVD disasters, the heavy assortment of disappointments could easily hinder running the "race marked out for us."

Every time athletes play one of these bad boys before a

game, they are dragging past anxieties back into the sports warehouse and psyching themselves out. Carrying a huge inventory of bad DVDs will mentally slow you down and make it impossible to run at game speed. Why do athletes hang on to anything that hinders their performance? If you are going to live in victory, it's time to lighten the load, so empty those shelves stacked with weighty expectations.

Jesus gave us the command "do not worry about your life" in Matthew 7:25. Yet, our mental warehouse is designed to store up a perception of our future situations. How can we reverse engineer the worrying process and start ditching the preconceived ideas that produce negative paralysis? Fortunately, the Bible offers real solutions to deal with inventory-control problems. With God's multi-dimensional skills, it is important to find the right verse that convinces the head and heart to let it go. God would love to assist you or anyone else in unloading your internal chaos without a nasty chorus of gagging in front of a toilet. The following is one of God's basic plans that calls for the arm muscles of an athlete. Just start your wind-up at the pitcher mound and make a special delivery.

***"Cast all your anxiety on him because he cares for you."***
1 Peter 5:7

With this strategy, the word "cast" describes your part in this pitch-and-catch clean-up. It requires you to grab every anxiety-filled recording you can think of and throw it to home plate. God is ready to assist by catching anything you throw at him.

This process of restoring your mental warehouse is no different from cleaning out the garage, your car, or a closet filled with junk. Only now you're dealing with worry and anxiety. It's up to you to choose something that your heart and mind will accept to symbolize your messed-up thoughts.

Then with God's help, take your garbage to the curb. All it takes is a little faith to make it happen.

***Faith is taking the first step even when you don't see the whole staircase.***
Dr. Martin Luther King Jr.

One way to show your faith is to transfer your anxious thoughts to DVDs and visualize them flying out of the sports warehouse like a tiny UFO invasion. Soccer players can imagine kicking a soccer ball of compacted anxiety into the goal with such force that it blows out the net. Golfers can use their practice swing to blast any nerves or hesitation out of the way. A friend of mine uses her "Babe Ruth moment" to deal with anxiety. Although she doesn't play on a team, she supplies one of the greatest baseball players in the history of the game with her negative thoughts or situations and visualizes him hitting them right out of the ballpark.

God doesn't want you to be defined by your mistakes, so take action and rid yourself of the negativity. Use any sports-related effort to throw, kick or hit your anxiety out of the park so your confidence can be restored. As a caring Father, God will see that you are serious about demonstrating your faith and handle whatever you throw at him, and as a warrior, annihilate any intergalactic threats.

If tossing DVDs seems too old school, what about downloading your anxious thoughts to a thumb drive? Or better yet upload to cloud storage. Be reminded that God created the original "cloud storage." His heavenly facility has unlimited space to hold the things in this life that have eternal value and offer a heavenly reward—eternal life. Maybe it's time to upgrade your IT (information technology) Department and gain access to your own private cloud. Since there are no restrictions when setting up an FTP (file transfer protocol) site, you can upload anxious thoughts from anywhere, anytime, and as often as you like. God can even accept your damaged and corrupted sports files at lightning-fast speeds.

God's private cloud offers the ultimate protection package. In Matthew 6:20 it says, "But store up for yourselves treasures in heaven, where moths and vermin do not destroy, and where thieves do not break in and steal." Plus, your cloud account maintains a complete biography of your life. Once you follow the bright light that leads to the afterlife; "each of us will give an account of ourselves to God" (Romans 14:12).

Most pro teams are so evenly matched that the outcome of a game is often determined by a buzzer-beater. During the last two minutes, something as simple as reading the game clock on the scoreboard can act like a stun grenade filled with desperation. Once the fear of defeat has blown-up the confidence of several athletes, that team will typically lose the game.

That doesn't have to be the case for you or your team. Even when the game clock is winding down, there is still time to "cast out" any last-second anxiety. God's purging strategy is available even when you're on the run. In the blink of an eye, God can help remove any explosive negativity without even calling a time-out. All you have to do is ask, toss, and it will be done.

***I can do all this through him***
***who gives me strength.***
Philippians 4:13

What if you made this clean-up approach into a 40-Day Challenge? And, what if the 40 days were up and the really tough fears were still going round and round inside your head? When everyone is counting on you to be the hero, the pressure can be unbearable.

If that is the case, the fear of making some type of stupid mistake may have an emotional attachment that is too strong to "cast out" or even drag out of the sports warehouse. Even though your prophetic disaster in front of fans may never happen, that doesn't seem to matter. That fear of repeating past mistakes can still take the knot in your stomach to the next level and keep you up all night tossing and turning. Don't be consumed by your past!

When your efforts to banish the pressure-filled fantasies are no longer effective, the scriptures offer an alternative game plan. Any big game regrets or insecurities that create fear are perceived as stumbling blocks, and before you know it, brick by brick, an insurmountable wall is formed inside your mind. Fear can use these walls to assemble a fortified structure the Bible calls a "stronghold." The walls of a stronghold symbolize something in your life that is standing in the way, too tall to climb, or too big to find a way around.

When it comes to sports, God has the power to change your sports warehouse into a stronghold that offers protection from negativity, whereas fear can build strongholds that will weigh you down and trap your God-given talent.

Don't let your mistakes become stumbling blocks. Even if they are cemented in place with a defeatist emotion, don't get discouraged—the battle is not lost. These strongholds can only hold you powerless if you let them. God can use the theater of your mind to set your captive heart free by demolishing any strongholds. Basically, his strategy to combat fears is similar to the one used by the African children who dreamed of being chased by a lion. They were told to alter their nightmare by stopping, turning around, and *fighting back* by screaming at the top of their lungs until the lion ran away. You have to change the plot in your fearful storyline to do the same: stop, turn, and fight.

When Goliath-sized situations show up to make you look bad, it's time to stand your ground instead of running away. Confiding with a friend or teammate may help build your confidence, but probably won't provide enough fire-power to complete your mission. Achieving success requires that you wage an emotional battle to stop the cycle of fear and paralyzing doubt. That means scripting a new and better story to play in the virtual reality of your mind. Only a captivating fight-to-the-end victory will change a nightmare into sweet dreams.

Before drafting your own story, let's look at God's epic battle against strongholds that symbolize your biggest fears. By adopting his strategy to your situation and with the right equipment, you can knock down any size stronghold. Running a wrecking ball on your own takes enormous faith, but that won't be a problem if you know whom to call.

***The weapons we fight with are not the weapons of the world. On the contrary, they have divine power to demolish strongholds.***
2 Corinthians 10:4

In this verse, the words "we fight" imply that the God of angel armies is with you, a member of your team, and supplying unstoppable weapons of destruction. Now you know why God wears so many hats (and helmets). His skills range beyond catching all your anxieties at home plate. So, anytime you feel trapped, or in a fight for your life, call in a prayer request for a divine demolition specialist. Admitting that you need help blasting your stubborn performance anxiety into pieces will speed up the approval process.

## The Mission

Anytime God shows up wearing his construction hard hat, you can expect the dynamite, wrecking balls, and bulldozers to be parked at the overhead doors of your mental warehouse. A major assault on strongholds of past and future failures is about to take place.

***You have broken through all his walls and reduced his strongholds to ruins.***

Psalm 89:40

Just because the walls of impending doom come tumbling down, don't think it's the end of the story. According to the Apostle Paul, demolishing strongholds is only one part of the clean-up process. It's time to soldier-up, so arm yourself with weapons from God's fear-busting arsenal and "wage war." Let's look at the complete passage in 2 Corinthians 10.

***"For though we live in the world, we do not wage war as the world does. The weapons we fight with are not the weapons of the world. On the contrary, they have divine power to demolish strongholds. We demolish arguments and every pretension that sets itself up against the knowledge of God, and we take captive every thought to make it obedient to Christ."***

2 Corinthians 10:3-5

As you hunt through the rubble in the sports warehouse, do you have any idea which thoughts you are about to take captive? Paul hints that we are to "demolish arguments and every pretension" that opposes God's plan. In other words, you are looking for any past game-changing mistakes that *argue* you're not good enough to be one of God's warriors and any thoughts that set up a "pretension" (claim) that you must be the hero. Dealing with the fear of failure, possible humiliation, and the pressure of perfection can feel like a death sentence. Those are the types of thoughts "we take captive" because they paralyze your God-given talent.

Choosing the right weapons from God's arsenal will determine the outcome of the mental battle. Which weapons will have enough divine firepower to take down fearful thoughts and hold them captive? When David faced his giant, he didn't back down. God had prepared him with a powerful weapon of emotion—raw courage. With that unstoppable level of confidence, David acknowledged that God would fight by his side as he faced his biggest, toughest fear—Goliath.

In the verse below, David's assault with verbal bullets may sound like overconfidence, but he was just keeping it real and letting everyone know that his heart was in the right place.

> ***This day the LORD will hand you over to me, and I'll strike you down and cut off your head. Today I will give the carcasses of the Philistine army to the birds of the air and the beasts of the earth, and the whole world will know that there is a God in Israel.***
>
> 1 Samuel 17:46

When you are attempting to silence your giant fears, don't be afraid to include some of David's powerful words and warrior attitude in your battle. Fear is a formidable emotion determined to rule the entire base of operations. Its traumatizing effects will maintain control until you set it straight. A mental victory will depend on your fighting skills. Be aware that logic struggles to beat powerful negative emotions. If you are to "take captive" a powerful fear, it takes a bigger and stronger positive emotion to tie it up. To seriously "wage war" will require locking and loading all three weapons of emotion: confidence, aggressiveness, and possessiveness.

The Apostle Paul writes that we should "take captive every thought to make it obedient to Christ." Why not use a storyline that knocks your giant fears down to size and chops off their heads like David did to Goliath? That is certainly more dramatic than dealing with individual captive thoughts and presenting them to Christ, but it will not eliminate the problem. With the Goliath method, the negative emotional tag has been defeated and separated from the situation, but it has not left the building. God knows your heart's pathological need to hold on to things you should "cast" out. God knows that if you are given half a chance "you will again" try to fill the emotional void and go back to your old bad habits. Without God's help, it would be all too easy to resuscitate your giant fears before the next game... but not if your prisoners are about to be shark bait

***"You will again have compassion on us; you will tread our sins underfoot and hurl all our iniquities into the depths of the sea."***

Micah 7:19

The word "tread" was commonly used in the phrase "treading of grapes," which is a metaphor for God's executing his wrath. God is using his wrath to restore your relationship with him by getting rid of sin. Sin includes things that damage a relationship. Fear can have a sinful nature if it keeps you from getting closer to God or interferes with his plan for you to develop perseverance.

Only you can write an epic story that guarantees success. If you're an athlete who thrives on emotion, it should be easy to relate to the plot in God's story. There is nothing like a fight that knocks out, stomps on, and forcibly removes your biggest fear. Why not direct a similar version of God's clobbering time? Have him going head-to-head with your biggest sports fears and using his powerful arm muscles to "hurl" all your iniquities into the nearest ocean. The force from hitting the water will either drown them or attract predators to finish them off for good.

But what are "iniquities"? They are the repeated offenses or sinful habits that separate you from God. In general, they are the total opposite of the "good things" that you would store up in your heart. Iniquities can include the type of emotion that not only damages your relationship with God but can also tear down a team. The list to post in the locker room includes hatred, jealousy, envy, selfish ambition, and fits of rage. You can find a more complete list of iniquities in Galatians 5:19-21.

To banish all the heart-racing anxiety from your base of operations means calling on God's power to identify and extract *all* the iniquities. This evil inventory must be dumped in a place so deep it can't be fished out. God's power will do that and begin to restore your sports inventory to a game-ready status.

To summarize, there are many ways to maintain a winning attitude before facing game-time challenges. When you look at what can hold you captive, know that God has the strength to kick down any walls standing in your way and the skills to surgically remove any sports drama. Whether you are a rookie dealing with confidence problems or a seasoned pro with "a state of constant anxiety," God has you covered.

The simple approach to reducing performance anxiety is to disarm the emotional tag. Adding a level of determined confidence to the situation will help fight back the paralyzing negativity. If that has very little effect, then you are dealing with stumbling blocks that need to be picked up and "cast out," even if it's one brick at a time. If you are facing a formidable stronghold that won't surrender, you will need God's relentless attitude to deliver the knock-out punch.

How an emotionally charged situation can last for years

is another mystery, but God's surgical expertise can instantly separate the hurtful emotion. Once the emotional tag is removed from the situation, he drowns it in the "depths of the sea" or places it "as far as the east is from the west" (Psalm 103:12). He then restores the emotional tag by attaching his peace, "which transcends all understanding" (Philippians 4:7).

Though there are things in life you wish you could forget, it is part of God's plan to leave the actual experience intact. That way, your pain can be a source of strength. When you learn from your brokenness, your story can be used to coach others without reliving the emotional sting.

Once the negativity is cleared out of the sports warehouse, the head and heart are back on the same team. Without the weight of anxiousness, you will have renewed energy. When the *entire* military base is transformed into a like-new status, extra space is available for the Holy Spirit to direct the next mission. The heart and mind can now "test and approve" God's perfect game plan and make it ready to execute.

> ***Do not conform to the pattern of this world, but be transformed by the renewing of your mind. Then you will be able to test and approve what God's will is—his good, pleasing and perfect will***
> Romans 12:2

If you have spent much time in church, you have surely met people who have faced tough circumstances in which they dropped the ball or fumbled big time in the game of life. Yet, they recovered by being transformed (renewed) from the inside out. Most of God's miracles take place in your mental warehouse. This is where we find his grace at work restoring the thoughts that bring down the hearts and minds of his believers. God is more than willing to bust up the old negative inventory and ship it out same-day-air.

When you're into sports, the higher the stakes, the more performance anxiety you will face. Preserving that positive transformation will take a daily effort to hunt down and exterminate all the "bad things" that creep back into a thought-crowded warehouse. Only then can you free up space for the "good things," such as God's word and his plan. The time and energy spent is definitely worth the reward. Life is better when you have the clarity to live within God's "good, pleasing, and perfect will."

# God's Time-Out

## Chapter 9

When Phil Jackson led the L.A. Lakers to their first championship, he started the season with a three-minute meditation, twice a day. The mental exercise was designed to help the team calm down, let go of all the distractions, and play with the type of clarity he called "living in the moment." Each day he gradually increased the time spent meditating, but not all the athletes responded. Some would sleep, some would stretch, but some were serious about the benefits.

How long should you put yourself in a time-out from humans and electronics? If you don't believe in the wisdom of a coach with eleven championship rings, how about the power of Oprah? She has enough money to hire a team of professionals to meditate for her, yet she says it takes her 20 minutes twice a day to find God.

***"Be still, and know that I am God."***

Psalm 46:10

If you have never spent time meditating, sitting still for a three-minute session can seem like solitary confinement. But you're not alone. Your heavenly Father is there to offer his perspective and clarity by guiding your thoughts. God knows more about the dynamics of the game than you think, and he is patiently waiting to share some prep time with you. He knows your heart and sees the daunting mess in the sports warehouse. God understands the challenges you will face, and he will provide all the basic "things" to get the job done. If you are serious about really getting to know God as your commanding officer, don't wait:

## Chapter 9

***But seek first his kingdom and his righteousness, and all these things will be given to you as well.***

Matthew 6:33

When God puts on his game face, the necessary sports "things" come right from his arsenal. Before he can hand out any weapons that are critical to your performance, he has to listen to the same defeatist attitude Phil Jackson heard on the way to another championship trophy. Once athletes find out that real meditation is all about tapping into God's dynamic energy, they might change their tune and take a time-out from their busy schedules. After all, God is at work, planning "mighty deeds" that need to be contemplated.

***"I will consider all your works and meditate on all your mighty deeds."***

Psalm 77:12

To better comprehend the need for daily meditation and the benefits of "living in God's moment," we must travel back in time for a brief history lesson.

The ancient Greek philosophers believed the human intellect was divided into two separate components. The mind is the intellectual side, the source of deep analytical thinking and wisdom, whereas the heart is the source of a wide variety of human emotions. Sound familiar? Athletes aren't the only ones dealing with a split personality.

The Bible also distinguishes the heart from the mind, treating them as distinctly different. More than 500 Bible verses are available to help coach the heart's emotional characteristics, both good and bad. On the other hand, only 114 verses talk about the mind, and only 15 discuss both.

These verses confirm that your heart, even off the field, is a serious influence in making major decisions. To make matters worse, the Bible also acknowledges that two heads are *not* better than one. There is an ongoing struggle between the heart and the mind.

When it comes to having the most issues, the heart is the odds-on favorite at a better than a four-to-one advantage. With all these issues comes a unique style in how to get things done. Competitive by design, when the head and heart are out of sync, they go at it like prizefighters in a boxing ring, each with exclusive fighting skills. Yet, the heart doesn't always fight fair.

***The heart is deceitful above all things and beyond cure. Who can understand it?***

Jeremiah 17:9

There is no cure for an evil heart, so the ongoing battle between the head and heart might never end. Even during peaceful times, the wounds don't heal. Fortunately, God understands the issues of a bad heart. He will always be there to help with the diagnosis and set up a treatment plan. Occasionally he even participates in open-heart surgery. If God didn't step in to better the odds, the mind would not stand a chance.

***I will give you a new heart and put a new spirit in you; I will remove from you your heart of stone and give you a heart of flesh.***

Ezekiel 36:26

When it comes to sports, why spend so much time and effort dealing with the issues of a "stony heart," especially when it can weigh you down with anxiety? Why not ignore its drama and hope it will leave you alone to play your own game?

As my sci-fi hero Mr. Spock would say, "That would be

most illogical." You cannot afford to ignore the heart because its competitive attitude can produce extraordinary performance and agility. Learn to manage its unpredictable behavior, and you will find that it can create awesome game-changing momentum.

***Above all else, guard your heart, for everything you do flows from it.***
Proverbs 4:23

My son was the high school quarterback in our small town. In his senior year, the coach had put together a team with state championship talent. During the playoffs, while holding on to a third quarter lead, our star running back went down with a game-ending injury. That was a turning point that triggered a swing in momentum: Suddenly, there was big trouble in maintaining a military mindset. When the offense came back to the huddle, it did not take a psychic to see what they were thinking–their confidence was in jeopardy. My son recognized the look of fear in his teammates' eyes. His plea for the guys to pull it together fell on deaf ears. The opposing team took the lead with the next score and the decline in the fans' enthusiasm confirmed that the strength to guard their hearts was gone. All the energy to bring home a state title was being unplugged—the command center was shutting down. Before the third quarter ended, the team had thrown away their unwavering confidence and replaced it with fear and passivity. A new sign was posted at the entrance of their military base of operations: **Closed for the Season**.

## Total Teamwork

The heart is usually given credit as the driving force behind a warrior's passionate performance. To wear the face of a warrior, however, you will need both head and heart working in sync, focused on the right goal. Only then will you achieve the level of intensity needed to stay in the zone and receive the payoff for all your hard work.

The reason the Bible separates the heart, and the mind is to show how powerful the emotions from the heart can be, and how the heart and mind can get over their issues to achieve God's plan. The greatest law in the Bible commands that the heart and mind work together, but it is rare to find evidence of that happening. Out of all the Bible verses that reference the heart and mind, such an alliance happened only once.

***All the believers were one in heart and mind. No one claimed that any of their possessions was their own, but they shared everything they had.***

Acts 4:32

When the heart and the mind are in rhythm, it resonates like a powerful subwoofer. Every person in Luke's account felt the need to share in the goal of becoming a winning church. In football, this type of camaraderie is also found in winning teams. A quarterback and a wide receiver can share this special connection, or a running back and the offensive line. As it works out, even if athletes have stored up to 10,000 hours worth of experiences in the sports warehouse, the strength of your team is determined by the depth of your relationships. The battle cry for any team pursuing a winning season should be: **"One heart, one mind, one dream, one team."**

The same collaboration holds true in the military base. If you are of one heart and mind, then everything runs smoothly, and you can expect to play a great game. The hard part is convincing both heart and mind that an alliance is required for success.

The biblical evidence indicates that the heart knows how to rule. When the heart overflows with extreme drama, the analytical mind is easily overpowered. The mind doesn't have the emotional weapons or the needed biblical training to put up much of a fight. The heart's ability to tie up the mind with an emotional rope always gains the advantage. Before long, the mind has lost its competitive attitude and is wrapped up with conflicting doubt and paralyzing indecision.

Proactive sports tags and tattoos can save the day. When the head and heart are encouraged with the right type of emotion and logic, both are pulled into resolving a sports situation. Without realizing it, this combination results in a collaboration of sustainable teamwork. Instead of sitting on the bench and letting your competitive head and heart fight it out, use the weapons in your arsenal to stay in the game and make a positive impact with teammates and on the scoreboard.

Is this heart-defeats-the-head battle starting to sound familiar? This ongoing struggle has been over-used by movie producers as a central storyline. Someone, almost always a woman, will be struggling to make a big emotional decision, but her logic for following through causes a teary-eyed conflict. Then the story takes a drastic turn when her heart realizes what it really wants and throws all reasoning out the church window. The ecstatic heart instantly triggers a run to fulfill its *destiny*, which of course is in the opposite direction, and to marry someone else. Guys, you should know this plot for runaway brides. Hollywood has scripted this "follow your heart" theme so many times it's in every chick flick to hit the big screen.

When it comes to money decisions, your heart always wants to spend more than your head says is in your wallet. The emotional thrill of buying something new overcomes the consequences of the purchase. Just ask any lottery winner who has won millions only to file for bankruptcy a few years later; his heart would not let him say no.

Still not convinced that heart-filled emotion devastates

common sense? Just look at the life of a politician. They are constantly being monitored by photographers and journalists to stay above reproach. Logic would dictate that if your last name was "Weiner," you would not be caught with your zipper down. And it would make sense to avoid any sexual drama, especially when using the power of social media. But that didn't stop former House Representative Anthony Weiner from the thrill of sexting on his cell phone. The bad press did, however, end his career in politics.

Jesus taught on many issues of the heart, but he didn't put the heart and mind together except when asked about the greatest commandment in the Bible. Then he clarified how both were needed to make a great relationship happen:

***"Love the Lord your God with all your heart and with all your soul and with all your mind and with all your strength."***

Mark 12:30

In this verse, we find the gold standard for achieving a united effort. When pursuing the greatest commandment, it will take more than just the power of your heart and mind working in sync. God wants you to bring it "all" into an act of worship. People who want an epic relationship with God must also include a soul (spiritual) connection. The same all-inclusive teamwork holds true when attempting to play your ultimate game or to accomplish any great undertaking. When all three entities answer the call to action, they become the catalyst for an explosive transformation and great things start to happen.

After dealing with the demands of the crowds, Jesus, even with all his spiritual strength, would frequently recharge by spending some quality time alone with God. God knows how to restore power to the heart and mind when we are overwhelmed. When you look at what holds you captive, know that God is ready to remove any performance anxiety before game time. Since the heart is deceitful, it's almost impossible to find its secret stash of negativity. It must be hiding on the subliminal level of the sports warehouse because you can feel the emotional disturbance. During that quiet time, ask for God's help. He can do more than just a Google search. He can tear the sports warehouse apart and has the authority to turn your "hidden person of the heart" upside down and empty his pockets of any fearful phobias.

***"Search me, O God, and know my heart; test me and know my anxious thoughts."***

Psalm 139:23

The sports benefit of "being in the moment" is that your heart is not backing down and playing it safe. When your heart is held hostage by anxious thoughts, it's easy to miss scoring opportunities that could close out the game, instead of letting the game's outcome be decided in the final seconds.

During your time-out with God, don't just relive the game situations that end in defeat, focus on letting them go: Get rid of them! As mentioned earlier, the mind is capable of making endless recordings, and the sports warehouse will grow to accommodate a sports arena, football stadium, or even a ski slope on the side of a mountain, but when it comes to heartfelt experiences the space is limited. Once someone reaches their maximum capacity, any negative baggage makes it almost impossible to "be in the moment." The ability to adjust on the fly is lost, and easy scoring opportunities are missed.

Being in God's moment is all about taking in your surroundings, such as enjoying a sunset, mountain range, or ocean view. It can also be about connecting with people in whatever situation they are going through. The Apostle Paul gives us a good example of "being in the moment" when we are with other people.

> ***Rejoice with those who rejoice; mourn with those who mourn. Live in harmony with one another.***
>
> Romans 12:15-16

## Unplugging a Bundle of Nerves

If your coach doesn't follow Phil Jackson's philosophy of meditating during practice, then it's up to you to make an appointment with God. Pre-game stress has a big effect on how you feel, so start by calming down, try to relax, and let go of the physical tension. When you feel stressed out, your muscles are fighting against each other to create pain, which means your muscle-control app has been corrupted. When this happens, some of your motor neurons are so revved-up that all your stored energy is being consumed and drains your emotional batteries before game time.

Since anxiety tightens your muscles to work against each other, consider adopting a stretching routine to put them back in harmony. Any type of light workout will make you aware of the few muscles that are out of sync. Stretching will reprogram all of your muscles to work together and neutralize the tension commonly stored in your shoulders, neck, and clenched jaw muscles.

Most corrupted muscle-control apps won't last against a 10-count of exercise, so if your stomach muscles are knotted up, do a set of 10 ab crunches to relax. Or, when seated on the long bus ride to the game, tighten your stomach muscles even tighter without moving, hold, and relax. If the first set of modified ab crunches doesn't unplug the tension, go for another round. It sounds crazy to create even more stress, but that's how you fight back.

As mentioned in chapter 7, breathing takes up a good chunk of your concentration. Controlled breathing can act as busywork to slow down your anxious heart. Success happens when you can train the mind to calm the heart and regain command of your military base. When you are caught without the time or place to seriously meditate with God, you can choose one of the many breathing techniques available to quiet overwhelming emotions. This one is about as simple as it gets, so adapt it to fit your needs.

Start by taking a moment to sit or stand still. If possible, close your eyes. This stops all the visual information from pouring into your brain, which shuts down the amount of tagging and recording taking place in the sports warehouse.

Next, focus on calming your racing heart by using a four-count. Take a deep breath through the nose on a 1-2 count and out the mouth on a 3-4 count. As you exhale, check the stress level in your neck by moving your head slowly from side to side.

Rotate your shoulders and let them drop. When your controlled breathing is enhanced with a 4-count, this high level of concentration changes the focus to an internal perspective and has a calming effect.

If you cannot sit still long enough to calm down hours before kickoff, it is time to do some mentally enhanced pacing to walk off your heart-racing apprehension. Save that overflow of adrenalin for the big game by synchronizing your breathing to work with a fast-walking four-count. Breathe in on steps 1-2, and then exhale on steps 3-4. Once your breathing and steps are synchronized, slow down your pace to slow down the emotional chaos racing through the command center.

Now that you have calmed down, see if you can unload some or all of your stressful sports inventory from the sports warehouse. God's help is available to remove any leftover fears, paralyzing doubts, and insecurities. Choose your favorite clean-up program, described in the last chapter, and the following verse will initialize your efforts.

***"The LORD will fight for you; you need only to be still."***

Exodus 14:14

Meditation is about making the world a better place, even if it's only inside your mind. Escaping to a quiet place is where God can effectively help you with some emotional management. Most people I know use some type of daily devotion to fill up their emotional reservoir with positive thoughts. Some of the greatest benefits, however, come from releasing unrealistic expectations. Many recommend "renewing your mind" first thing in the morning (see Matthew 6:33, page 140) before the caffeine kicks in or before your head starts spinning with the demands of the day.

Because of its benefits, meditating is one of the habits of highly successful people. They want a clear head to avoid costly mistakes that could affect their lives and the lives of others. Even if your day doesn't require making million-dollar decisions, why not try it anyway? Set a goal to make it one of your daily habits. When your head and heart are united, you can be in God's moment, ready for anything.

# The Micro-Warrior

## Chapter 10

Even after 20 years as the starting quarterback for the Green Bay Packers, Brett Favre said the thrill of scoring points never got old. And it showed. At 40 years old, every time he threw a touchdown pass, his face lit up as if he had just unwrapped the perfect present. He could not contain his excitement.

What is going on when a quarterback displays more enthusiasm than his biggest fans? Why did Favre celebrate every touchdown as if a surprise birthday party had erupted in the football stadium? That competitiveness, driven by overwhelming emotion, is why Favre was miles apart from athletes who need an intellectual mindset. A heartfelt passion drove him to greatness.

Surely you have heard the expression, "You can tell the age of the boy by the price of the new toy." Or you've heard people talk about the little boy who is trapped inside a grown man's body. That little guy is commonly referred to as the "inner child" or "man-child." He stays small, out of the way most of the time, but when the game is on, he runs around the command center, acting tough until you see him go nuts, celebrating big time after great plays. Since your sports buddy can help you play with the heart of a superhero, a more fitting title for him would be the *micro-warrior*.

When a defensive player makes a big play, his personality transforms. His level of excitement reaches a point where the micro-warrior takes over his body language. He can no longer walk in a straight line. He has no choice but to do a combination of hops, skips, and leaps while taking an erratic path to the sidelines.

Another true warrior who left fans in a state of awe was Walter Payton, running back for the Chicago Bears.

## Chapter 10

Walter was often known as "Sweetness." Why would such a tough athlete have such a sugary nickname? Payton's brother explained that the nickname was meant to pick on his soft, high-pitched voice, but it quickly became a badge of honor. The media was happy to promote Payton's nickname because, as one reporter said, "He runs so sweet that it gives me cavities just watching him."

Walter was the exception when it came to athletes who need extreme repetition. Walter didn't need 10 touches to get into the flow of the game. He would say, "One hit and I'm ready!" He was right; his numbers backed him up. All it took was one good tackle to ring his bell, and he came out swinging. It was a wake-up call for his micro-warrior to get in the game.

Then watch the fun begin as Sweetness began wearing down the defense. During the years when the Bears had a bumbling offense, fans would joke that there were only two plays in the Bears' playbook: Payton run right, and Payton run left. It did not matter if Walter had a good or bad offensive line that year. Game after game he would grind out a consistent 4.4 yards per carry in a career that lasted 13 years and totaled over 16,000 rushing yards.

Off the field, Walter was famous for his dance moves and many pranks with fireworks. His dance moves were so impressive that he became one of the finalists in a dance competition held by the TV show *Soul Train*. In his autobiography *Never Die Easy*, he recalled a statement by his good friend and teammate Roland Harper, who described Walter this way:

> ***"I think he loved M-80s because they were the loudest. One time he set one off in the lobby of our training camp in the middle of the night. It was during two-a-days, so everyone was exhausted. The police and fire departments came, and the police***

***knew Walter had done it, so they went to his room. By the time they got there, he had snuck out a window and had set the sirens on their cars off."***

Roland Harper

Another Bears teammate, Mike Singletary, says, "I always had to be alert when I was around him because he might tie your shoestrings to a chair. The party was never dull with him here."

When an athlete blasts the locker room with music from an oversized boom box and has a reputation for endless laughter, practical jokes, and vitality—an emotional micro-warrior has come out to play. Only a rare and fatal liver disease would diminish Walter's unlimited energy. His passion for celebrating life ended far too soon at the age of 45.

## Making that Spiritual Connection

The man-child's momentary emotional appearance has been noted for centuries. Psychologists have filled bookstore shelves with all sorts of names and profiles to describe your alter ego, but does God acknowledge his existence? Definitely! The Bible includes numerous verses to describe his predictable good and bad qualities. These verses not only help to manhandle your own little buddy in daily life, but also predict his emotional behavior when he wears the face of a warrior.

In chapter 2 we indirectly referred to the mini-sports buddy as the tiny "hidden person of the heart." In the following verse, the Apostle Paul warns how your extra set of eyes can take you on an ego trip (ego = **E**dging **G**od **O**ut) and take your laser focus off what is really important. This passage was written to a group of believers who were surrounded by religious fanatics just as extreme and vocal as any sports fans in a packed stadium.

## Chapter 10

***I pray that the eyes of your heart may be enlightened in order that you may know the hope to which he has called you, the riches of his glorious inheritance in his holy people, and his incomparably great power for us who believe.***

Ephesians 1:18-19

This was part of Paul's encouragement to the believers in Ephesus. The emotion was so overwhelming that they could no longer see the big picture of God's game plan and were starting to lose heart. They needed to refocus "the eyes of the heart" to see the "incomparably great power" God had made available.

So according to multiple verses in the Bible, your micro- warrior is a part of your heart. Your fun-loving, thrill-seeking mini sports buddy also has access to unlimited power. He can choose to build good and bad strongholds and wear a jetpack to lift you up or fill a backpack with enough trouble to weigh you down. With this new insight, we can better utilize the powerful role of the heart and develop better teamwork between the heart and mind. Let's take a second look at this heart verse, written by King Solomon.

***Above all else, guard your heart, for everything you do flows from it.***

Proverbs 4:23

This concept depicts a no-nonsense military presence at the entrance of your base of operations. Who is responsible for 24-hour guard duty? That would be *you*. It's your analytical mind's job to be the Military Police and ensure moral standards are followed. With opposing forces struggling to take control, be sure to screen everything with God's values to keep the micro-soldier from defecting to the dark side. This is no easy task when a deceitful heart can justify bending or even breaking all the rules. Just how much mischief can a little person of the heart get into anyway?

> ***For out of the heart come evil thoughts—murder, adultery, sexual immorality, theft, false testimony, slander.***
> Matthew 15:19

Forget the guard duty, with a list of potential crimes this long, maybe you should lock up the little stinker and throw away the key! Unfortunately, you cannot keep him behind bars and expect him to become the ultimate warrior right before game time. So, it is best to guard your heart, and as the Apostle Paul described on page 25, "Every athlete exercises self-control in all things." That way you can avoid any potential pitfall before it trips you up and brings everything good in your life crashing down.

No coach—regardless of how many Super Bowl rings he is wearing—can win without motivating you to play your best. Think of the head-and-heart relationship in the same way. Your head needs to coach your heart. But realize that the heart still has full control of all the weapons in the armory, and it doesn't take much for him or her to become trigger-happy. If you are to take charge of the micro-warrior's extreme emotions and create a tenacious attitude to win, you *must* know who you are dealing with.

Ever heard your friends say, "When are you going to act your age?" or "Why don't you just grow up?" If so, it was because your micro-buddy was not using age-appropriate behavior.

Just how old is this fun-loving micro-entity anyway? Judging from the way game show contestants light up when winning a prize, and how the grandpas have to prove their masculinity to young skirts, the micro-man doesn't age. He must be caught somewhere between a man and a boy, which would explain a good deal of teenage behavior. Will he always be stuck in middle school or a frat-house time loop? Probably, so it is vital to cover the coaching skills you will need to handle your ageless micro-athlete.

Anyone who has coached young athletes knows the challenge of keeping them on task. They have trouble switching on their laser focus because they are easily distracted. The micro-warrior is constantly looking to be entertained, and it's all about extreme emotion. One minute the micro-warrior can turn it up and go full Rambo for you. Then, after a wink from the cheerleaders, he will melt into a love-smitten Romeo. If he turns to the dark side, it only takes a small amount of negativity for him to psych you out. This unpredictable variety of overwhelming drama requires you to *keep him busy.*

At practice, it shouldn't be a problem to keep the micro-warrior occupied. Just because logic is not the magic bullet in his mental game it's still useful for personal entertainment. The clarity that comes from seeing the big picture can be used to fire sports tattoos at boring game film or to enhance scrimmages. This type of busywork adds more awesome "follow your heart moments" to his collection of sports DVDs.

Of course, the head coach and assistant coaches have their own ideas on how to keep your head and heart busy during every minute at practice. But what about time spent off the field, between the last practice and the upcoming game? The travel time of a road game or even the downtime of a home game can make the minutes drag by slower than a herd of turtles racing to the finish line. Sure, you can study the playbook or more game film, but at his age, there is a limit to how much pre-game information the micro-warrior can absorb before zoning out. How can you not go stir crazy?

Retired NBA legend Shaquille O'Neal has broadened his skills and become a sports analyst. In an interview, he reminisced about killing time during one of his playoff runs.

> ***"I would calm my nerves with a playlist ready with the hottest rap songs out there and bob my head,***

***think about the game and relax. Then the game would start and I'd put my angry face on."*** Shaquille O'Neal

Michael Phelps became the most decorated Olympic athlete of all time by breaking the record for the most medals. He closed out his swimming career at the 2016 Rio Olympics with 23 gold medals, 28 overall. The old record was 18, and it stood for 48 years, which means the new record may never be broken.

As TV cameras tracked his every move near the pool, Phelps always stood out from the crowd of swimmers because of his huge headphones. Like Shaq, Phelps found that music was the best way to separate himself from performance anxiety. He would not give his micro-warrior a single minute before the starting gun to think things to death and mess up the sports warehouse. That way, Phelps could focus on one thing: going for the gold.

Judging by the way a hidden person of the heart can keep a song going around in your head, music ranks right up there with binging on munchies when you're not even hungry. Even when enduring a boring exercise routine, music can make the time fly by. Being entertained by favorite tunes is a positive low-calorie distraction that will keep your head and your heart emotionally busy hours before game time.

## Think with a Pencil

To escape from reality, many athletes go for fun and easy brain games. Michael Jordan might play with a lot of heart-racing emotion, but his micro-warrior didn't appear to dominate his mindset. Still, Jordan understood the importance of keeping him under control. His love for crossword puzzles kept his warrior heart busy. If you hate spelling but enjoy simple low-tech pencil games, Sudoku and other number puzzles may work for you. Their popularity has grown to fill the magazine racks at grocery and bookstores.

Pick out a few of the pencil and/or electronic brain games from the hundreds available. They can provide an enjoyable distraction. Choose games that are tough enough to be a challenge. The micro-warrior loves competition, so don't hesitate to pick the games that can actually beat you, such as computer chess. Such games offer a sense of reward when you win and a reality check when you lose. Whether you choose high or low-tech games, they should consume enough of your concentration to shut out that hyper-anxiety of the sports world and let you experience being lost in your own little world.

## Talk! Talk! Talk!

Using "self-talk" has become a popular way of keeping the stress of everyday living from being overwhelming. Everyone maintains this constant internal commentary, but in the world of sports a heavy dose of clear positive affirmations is required. Reassuring advice can also combat the insecurities that keep athletes tossing and turning the night before a big game, especially one that rivals Super Bowl expectations.

The reason self-talk works is because you are actually self-coaching the micro-warrior. A coach at any level knows that wrong thinking ends with wrong behavior, and that can be devastating to achieve victory. To avoid that wrong thinking, use positive self-coaching both on and off the field. Keep the affirmations simple enough to guide your young micro-warrior through a complicated or uncomfortable task yet offer encouraging words to maintain the confidence of a warrior. Limit your self-talk so you can focus on your job. Let someone else sweat the details, such as worrying about the scoreboard.

A sports relationship with your inner warrior is more complicated than just acknowledging its existence. Even the top professional athletes struggle with the delicate balance between the structure and the freedom needed to keep their micro-warrior in the zone. During the 2013 NBA playoffs, LeBron James was interviewed by *USA Today* about his struggle with winning the mental game. He said:

> ***"Sometimes it works great,***
> ***sometimes it doesn't," he said.***
> ***"Sometimes it can cloud my mind too***

> ***much and I get to thinking about the game too much instead of just playing. Sometimes I'm able to put myself in situations that are better for me and better for our team by knowing what happened before.***
>
> ***"I guess it's a gift and a curse."***
>
> LeBron James

In Michael Jordan's book *For the Love of the Game: My Story,* he talks about dealing with his overwhelming passion during games and keeping it under control.

> ***"I would look for easy opportunities to set the tone, to settle my mind, so I could let the game come to me instead of chasing it all night. That's one of the differences between a good player and a great one."***
>
> Michael Jordan

With the outcome of so many pro games—even world championship games—being decided in the last two minutes, there is no time for mediocrity. Both LeBron and Michael have struggled to avoid closing out games with costly mental errors. It was LeBron's out-of-control curiosity that gets the best of him. He felt that if questioning game situations is good, then more is better. When athletes have too many unresolved questions or too many options, it ends up causing a paralyzing cloud of confusion. Information overload can change the "gift that keeps on giving" into the Grinch's curse that steals your game.

Jordan knows that you need to play hard to win. When the pressure builds, trying *too hard* creates a chokehold. Now the micro-warrior can't catch his breath and is forced right out of the military base. He ends up pouting or hating the game until Michael steps back, loosens his death-grip, and embraces the flow of the game. This restores the competitive freedom to create scoring opportunities—just by letting the game come to him. Michael is right. When it comes to reaching your true potential, the difference between a good player and a great one is the ability to stop, step back from the game, and let the game come to you.

## Slip of the Tongue

Head coaches, athletes, and even the reclusive micro-warrior love to talk: "For the mouth speaks what his heart is full of." Regardless of the source, it is easy to slip up. When the micro-warrior's mental state flips from being a gift to a curse, the root cause is his literal interpretation of orders from the Strategic Command Center. Taking everything literally should not be a big deal. Your logical mind knows what it wants to accomplish, but your heart rules, and the rules change when running at game speed. A simple slip of the tongue can result in fatal repercussions instead of huge rewards.

When preparing to face tough teams, your self-talk or even real talk to other players should avoid some seemingly innocent affirmations. Although the simple expression "I have to ..."—as in "I have to play my best game ever in the playoffs" or "I have to make the tackle" or "I have to score points to win"—*sounds* like the right thing to say before or during a game, in the micro-warrior's world it is another story. When emotions run high, what you think you're saying to coach your micro-warrior is not what he hears. This type of affirmation raises the stakes to the next level by adding an enormous amount of pressure. He is hearing that he must generate a super-hero performance ... *or else*. It is the same as saying, "I have to save the little girl from the burning building, or else." Unless he can comply with your game plan, he is literally facing a life-or-death situation. By simply changing "I have to..." into "I want to...," your self-fulfilling prophecy becomes words of encouragement and support, and your micro-warrior will excel to make it come true.

Ultimately, try to eliminate the word "not" and any of its contractions such as "can't," "don't," or "won't." When you use affirmations such as "I won't drop this pass" or "I can't miss this shot" or "I am not striking out," it sets up the micro-warrior to organize and execute what *not* to do. Even starting a sentence with, "What if I..." opens a self-fulfilling prophecy that tends to be negative. It instructs the micro-warrior to grab a past screw-up and drag it into the sports warehouse. Any phrase that describes what *not to do* creates confusion. Your words have created a stun grenade that implies failure, which all circles back to the number-one rule in the military base: "Mentally organize what you need to execute."

If you do have a slip of the tongue, you must correct these negative affirmations by adding some positive coaching instructions. When you are focused on a "can do" attitude, it will bring a "can do" result. It is not that hard to step back and use statements of encouragement like, "This is my job" or "This is what I want to do" and "I have done this before." Then take Michael Jordan's advice and let the game come to you.

Earlier we worked on a series of sports tattoos for a wide receiver to find the handle on the football. These are great coaching tools to inspire the micro-warrior to produce an extraordinary performance. There is, however, one last sports tattoo that completes this series. This one engages a momentary shot of adrenalin for a burst of speed. It is needed for a receiver to create separation from the defender or gain a couple of extra inches to reach for the ball. After the catch, it can be used to break tackles, and as in many sports, a shot of adrenalin is needed to outrun the competition.

Adrenalin is a hormone that can give you incredible strength but is not without dangerous side-effects. If it were a prescription drug, the warning label would read, "To avoid a sports injury, use only when supervised by trained coaches. You are not indestructible."

In chapter 1, we were looking for that "something extra" that happens under the hood when an athlete's mental game is hitting on all cylinders. Now we've found it. The spark needed to rev up the micro-warrior with *an unstoppable passion* has four wheels.

## Take the Driver's Seat and Floor It!

As you can see, that pristine showroom shine is long gone. No need to worry about door dings. This modified muscle car from the 1970s is designed for a physical type of racing. It can bump and run with the best and, if caught, take or make a good hit.

When customizing this sports tattoo, be sure to include

a rewarding masculine side. Its overall power is determined by how much adrenalin it pumps into your veins. *So, choose a car you are passionate about. Personalize your dream car with a custom paint job, beefed-up engine, and just the right accessories to excite your warrior's heart.*

To be effective, adapt this sports tattoo to your game and make sure it contains enough fundamental skills to go with the heartfelt response. The driving package for football players includes a deer guard that resembles a face mask for personal protection, and a set of high-beam headlights for a panoramic view of the play. The air scoop feeds extra oxygen to a turbo-charged motor. The increased airflow means increased horsepower, and under the hood, it is up to you to create a motor that would go from 0 to 60 instantaneously.

The matchstick wipers are a reminder to switch on the high-speed matching process to read the play and react, even during extreme weather conditions. It's also important to have the right drivetrain and tires when playing on real turf. Add the optional all-wheel-drive package for wet weather conditions, or even switch out the tires and add metal studs for muddy or snowy games.

The off-road seatbelt harness is a reminder to put safety first. There is nothing wrong with putting an extra shot of adrenalin into making a big hit, but do it the right way. Buckle up and use the proper tackling techniques to avoid broken bones or a head-on, season-ending concussion. The flames out the tailpipe are a reminder to feel the power. Listen to that deep rumble at idle, before revving up the motor to a deafening scream. Need even more power to energize every muscle? Install a turbo-boost button that releases a blended mix of nitro-fuel but hang on and use it at your own risk.

A momentary burst of adrenalin can be used to avoid someone or push someone out of the way. That is why this sports tattoo is also designed to tie into weight-room workouts. If you can move 300+ pounds in the weight room, why not do it on the football field? Before visualizing your muscle car assisting in weight-room workouts, consult a certified weightlifting coach. Trying to do too much, too soon, is dangerous.

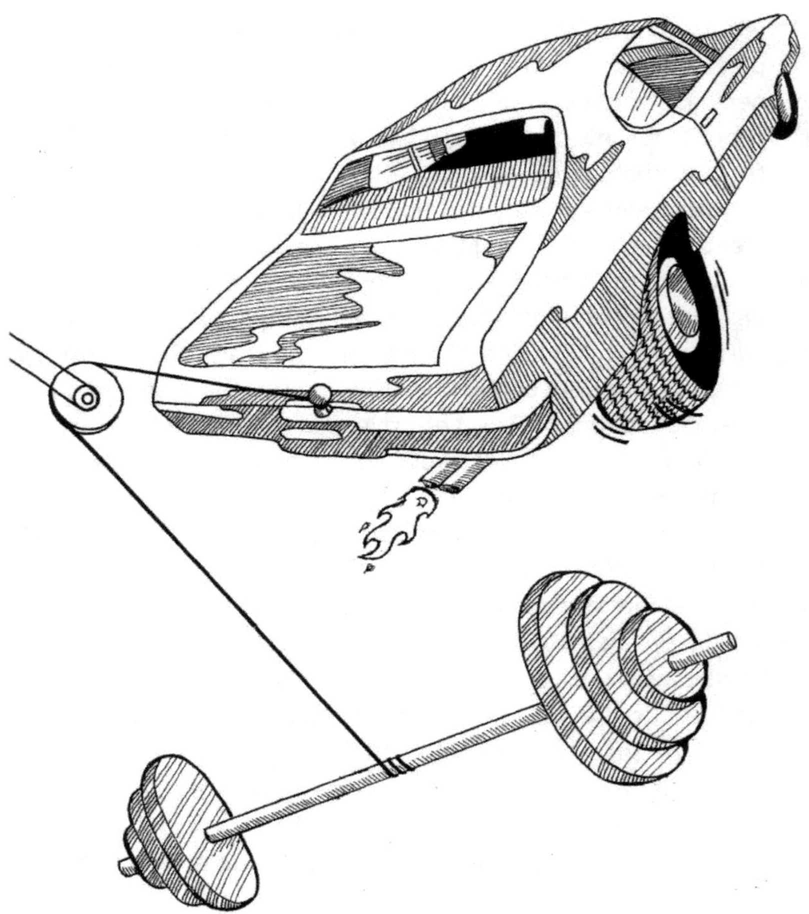

**Hit the Gas, Feel the Horsepower!**

All race cars have a tachometer to measure the engine's RPM (revolutions per minute). Motors are designed to reach maximum horsepower at a certain RPM. There is a point on the display where the RPM numbers change from white to red, commonly referred to as the "red line." Exceeding the red line risks causing damage to the engine or a blown motor. The same holds true for the human body. When this sports tattoo is triggered by revving up the motor to a deafening scream and burning the tires, don't exceed the red line. Seek the help of a certified personal trainer to determine your limits.

## Post-Game Review

The Bible covers many insightful characteristics that can be used as motivation in coaching the micro-warrior. One of the many verses speaks of the micro-warrior's love of hunting for treasure. When you tag something as valuable, such as the football, it becomes a prized possession, and the micro-warrior will be focused like a laser beam on acquiring it.

***"For where your treasure is, there your heart will be also."***

Matthew 6:21

We have covered numerous hunting weapons that God has designed to glorify his kingdom. Since the "eyes of your heart" see what you see, be careful whom you target. Powerful weapons should be aimed at the right people in accordance with God's plan. They are not to be used as little boy toys to scope out the next cheerleader Barbie. Disciplined coaching of these powerful weapons shows that you are ready to join what David called "the armies of the living God."

# Greatest Commandment in Sports

## Chapter 11

It wasn't accidental that sports became a big part of your life. Although being an athlete doesn't require the courage of a David and Goliath deathmatch, God can use a public display of competitiveness for spiritual development. If you are to be his representative at sporting events, he wants you to be a complete athlete, prepared with the courage to face any type of adversity.

As with any father figure or head coach, God's expectations are high because he perceives great potential. To understand God's perspective, we have covered countless Bible verses that contain information, inspiration, promises, and commandments. Hopefully, a few of the verses have stuck with you and can help you to experience contentment as described in Philippians 4:11-12 and "have life and have it abundantly" John 10:10 (ESV). Out of all the verses we have covered, which are the most important? Is there one you would call the greatest commandment?

A couple of thousand years ago, Jesus, as a teacher of God's word, was faced with those same questions from religious leaders. When crowds gathered to hear Jesus speak, Jewish factions would become jealous and frequently looked for ways to embarrass and discredit him. One of the Pharisees tested him by asking, "Of all the commandments, which is the most important?" Jesus replied:

***"Love the Lord your God with all your heart and with all your soul and with***

***all your mind and with all your strength. The second is this: 'Love your neighbor as yourself.' There is no commandment greater than these."***

Mark 12:30-31

If this first verse looks familiar, you have heard it at church or know it from reading the Bible. Or you might recall it from chapter nine when we looked at the head and heart rivalry. Basically, the greatest commandments are mission statements directing us to execute God's game plan. That means you are called to transform lives. Once God helps you restore the specialized talents of your head and heart, you will have the strength to influence the hearts and minds of your neighbors. But undertaking God's mission will take even more—a strong spiritual connection with one's soul. When God's Holy Spirit is a part of the formula, the power of "love" becomes the catalyst to success. It's a piece of the puzzle that combines all three entities "together in perfect unity."

***And over all these [Godly] virtues put on love, which binds them all together in perfect unity.***

Colossians 3:14

When pursuing the greatest relationship with God, Jesus said it won't be easy when you see how "narrow the road [is] that leads to life" (Matthew 7:14). During the journey, it will take all your strength and a whole lot of love to keep the over-emotional heart, the detail-oriented mind, and even the idol-chasing soul from running you off the road and crashing in the ditch. God's biblical guard rails offer protection from major disasters, but still, life's sinful distractions will show up as easy exits and side-track your journey away from God's greatest rewards.

After Jesus recited the greatest commandments, an expert in Jewish law tried to trip him up by asking for clarification on the second commandment: "And who's my neighbor?" (Luke 10:29). Jesus responded by telling the famous parable of the Good Samaritan. A parable is a short fictional story where one of the characters represents God and another character is someone we find relatable. The plot is commonly used to illustrate a spiritual principle. The most memorable stories will seem real and generate long-lasting emotions. That may be why Jesus incorporated 40 parables into his teachings to impact the hearts and minds of his followers.

Everyone knows the meaning of a "Good Samaritan." It's a person who goes out of their way to participate in an "act of kindness." We even have laws to protect those who act as Good Samaritans and administer medical attention after a car accident. What really makes Jesus' Good Samaritan story impactful was the underlying subplot. Jesus would expose the mindset of the Jews and their religious leaders toward Samaritans.

The Samaritans, as you might have guessed, lived in Samaria, a place to avoid because it was on the wrong side of the tracks. They were considered to be an inferior race of foreigners and religious heretics. It was common knowledge that they had been enemies for hundreds of years. In fact, because of their history, Jews would not talk or even associate with Samaritans because they were considered "unclean."

This is the biblical story of the Good Samaritan.

***In reply Jesus said: "A man was going down from Jerusalem to Jericho, when he was attacked by robbers. They stripped him of his clothes, beat him and went away,***

***leaving him half dead. A priest happened to be going down the same road, and when he saw the man, he passed by on the other side. So too, a Levite, when he came to the place and saw him, passed by on the other side. But a Samaritan, as he traveled, came where the man was; and when he saw him, he took pity on him. He went to him and bandaged his wounds, pouring on oil and wine. Then he put the man on his own donkey, brought him to an inn and took care of him. The next day he took out two denarii and gave them to the innkeeper. 'Look after him,' he said, 'and when I return, I will reimburse you for any extra expense you may have.'"***

***"Which of these three do you think was a neighbor to the man who fell into the hands of robbers?"***

***The expert in the law replied, "The one who had mercy on him."***

***Jesus told him, "Go and do likewise."***

Luke 10:30-37

This story reveals how the second commandment is like the first. When someone helps one of God's children, it is as if they are helping God himself. Something as simple as going to church and extending a helping hand beyond your circle of close friends are both acts of love that become acts of worship. God finds both pleasing because they accomplish his will. The similarities continue with the need to use the unique expertise of your head and your heart to accomplish great things. In this case, it's about loving God by loving your neighbor.

In order for the Samaritan to do the right thing, he would need to stop for the injured man, and use the skills of his heart and mind. Treating the man's wounds and transporting him to a safe place would be the logical mind's area of expertise; however, before performing these acts of love an internal alarm would go off. The wounded man could have been a robber setting a trap or he could be a Jew who would rise up and attack him out of hatred. There were plenty of reasons for the Samaritan to ignore the situation and walk on by.

This story illustrates how your mind's logic can struggle with the heart and soul's compassion. If faced with a similar situation, your heart would have to overrule the mind and disregard a mental warehouse full of reasons to avoid someone in trouble. It was that "follow your heart moment" that triggered the teamwork needed to execute God's greatest commandments.

When using the specialized talents of your head and heart to help someone who is struggling, don't expect it to be easy, and don't expect to be rewarded. Love often moves you to go the extra mile even if it's outside your comfort zone. When it comes to sports, an act of loving your neighbor might require sharing encouraging words with a teammate who had a bad game or helping a confused rookie adjust to a new level of intensity. Anytime you extend a helping hand, it opens the door for the recipient to ask "Why?" and wonder about your motive. Then you can explain how you're on the road to obeying one of the greatest commandments ever written.

The last command to "Love your neighbor as yourself" actually ties into the first commandment. The concept of using your heart, mind, and soul to love God, also trickles down to helping your neighbor and loving yourself. You were created to love and be loved by God. If you don't feel accepted by God, then it's time to take a personal evaluation of your own heart, mind, and soul. What will it take for each of these entities to feel loved so they can express God's love? Don't misunderstand, loving yourself is not about being self-centered. In God's eyes, this type of self-love is about following the Golden Rule in Luke 6:31: "Do to others as you would have them do to you." That means not cutting corners but investing in yourself just as you would invest in the betterment of someone else. Loving yourself also means staying "Golden" in your mental warehouse. How can you love your neighbor or yourself if you're guilty of keeping a personal hate-list? When your heart is in a good place, it's easy to lend a helping hand.

As we found out, when you spend time meditating, God can fix heart issues. He is an excellent surgeon, and you are preapproved for treatment. God even has the expertise to "give you a new heart and put a new spirit in you" (Ezekiel 36:26) so you can better love yourself. Plus, God has the skills to help you clean-up the chaos in your thought-crowded warehouse so you can be "in the moment," God's moment, ready to respond to someone in need.

Besides the Good Samaritan story, the Bible has numerous guidelines to put the power of your heart, mind, and soul to work toward a common goal. Earlier we looked at the process of acquiring wisdom from the following verses; now let's take a second look to reveal the big picture.

> ***Consider it pure joy, my brothers and sisters, whenever you face trials of many kinds, because you know that the testing of your faith produces perseverance. Let perseverance finish its work so that you may be mature and complete, not lacking anything. If any of you lacks wisdom, you should ask***

***God, who gives generously to all without finding fault, and it will be given to you. But when you ask, you must believe and not doubt, because the one who doubts is like a wave of the sea, blown and tossed by the wind. That person should not expect to receive anything from the Lord. Such a person is double-minded and unstable in all they do.***

James 1:2-8

If 100 people were surveyed, how many would respond with the battle cry of "Oh joy!" when facing "trials of many kinds"? This type of heartfelt emotion may sound inappropriate, but the biblical version of "joy" is a constant sense of well-being. It's a feeling of contentment that stays with you. This type of "joy" is a reminder not to let uncomfortable situations steal the feeling of being in good company with God by your side.

From a warrior's perspective, it also describes the personal satisfaction of having the sword of the Spirit in your possession and the feeling of being hand-picked by God for a special mission—to grow your faith. Only after facing a challenging situation will you part with the baby steps and stand tall as a soldier who is "mature and complete."

Like a number of teachings on personal development, this verse in the first chapter of James is coaching your head and heart about faith and perseverance. When a sports situation turns into a knock-down, out-of-control battle, it is not the time to lose confidence and retreat. It is time to have some faith and trust in God's unrivaled power. Fighting back with great faith and the sword of the Spirit will develop perseverance, and perseverance is what triggers a hang-in-there, don't-quit attitude in a come-from-behind victory.

Beating the odds will also require wisdom, and God has

a generous supply, but you have to ask for it. Sometimes it takes calming down before asking. Once the emotional heart is out of the way, the mind can use wisdom to strategize a better solution. At other times, the heart needs wisdom to know when to turn up the competitive emotion. If the head or heart can't work together when defeat looks obvious, the indecision results in athletes' becoming "double-minded and unstable in all they do."

Both of the greatest commandments use love as the primary emotion to trigger the act of love. In fact, we are called to "Do everything in love" (1 Corinthians 16:14), but how can love act as an explosive word grenade to transform one's athletic ability?

Phil Jackson said that most pro basketball players live in a state of constant anxiety. Then there was Michael Jordan ... overflowing with a love for the game. In TV interviews, he often mentioned his love of basketball. Why? Did he love the competitiveness, playing with his teammates, or just the challenge and thrill of victory?

As it turns out, Michael's love for the game was not a warm and fuzzy feeling like opening a heart-shaped box of chocolates on Valentine's Day. It is a powerful emotion people share when creating a special bond. Michael's sports-love was the super glue for greatness. Not only did it cement together the hearts and minds of his teammates, but it would bind together his heart, mind, and soul as well. When Michael added a sports-love to his game, the entire team would reap the rewards of winning championship trophies.

Can another athlete's love for the game influence your skills? What if Air Jordan or your favorite superstar wanted you as his teammate in a pickup game? How impressive would that be! The experience would deepen your love of the game and that love might become all-consuming. What if you perceived God as your partner in your pursuit of the game? His abilities are way beyond any superstar status. Wouldn't a sudden awareness of his presence also empower a starry-eyed love for the game?

Our DNA is wired with a need to be connected to something greater. Even if your competitive skills never leave the driveway in front of your house, a superstar's arrival would charge up your game. The hard part is convincing you that God's love generates more unlimited power and energy than you can imagine. There is no reason why he can't be your go-to guy for influencing a stellar performance. His presence will always be with you because he will always pick you as his teammate. With him by your side, you can be a part of something greater that influences a personal love for the game.

Jesus said, "In this world you will have trouble" (John 16:33). When you least expect it, a flat tire, running out of gas, or some other major distraction in life will make it hard to drive on that narrow road towards completing God's greatest commandments. That is why it's so important to spend time alone with God working on your sports inventory. The head and heart can change their attitudes after every play, but quickly return to a game-ready status if your sports warehouse is anchored to withstand the storm. When your clean-up efforts create enough room to turn things around, it's easy to gain a second perspective, "God's perspective," and be "in God's moment," ready to achieve his greatest commandments in sports.

What is your sports version of the greatest commandment? Would it read something like this: "Pursuing the greatest things in life is all about getting the best out of your heart, mind, and soul." It will take God's assistance to create a love that unifies your game-time performance."

# The Final Battle

## Chapter 12

In every hard-fought battle, it's all about using your mental warehouse to inspire the heart, mind, and soul. Will the heart and mind be satisfied to work in harmony to face the challenge, or will there be conflict? Will one or both ignore the soul or help it find a deep spiritual connection? And what about fulfilling God's game plan? Will anyone of the three doubt their ability to remain strong and terminate any threats to shut down the entire military base of operations? Any disunity can sound the retreat before the battle even begins.

Although Jesus faced many battles during his ministry, he never hesitated to follow through on God's plan. His heart and mind maintained a unity that would always prevail. Yet, at the end of his ministry, when called to fulfill a purpose greater than himself, we find Jesus filled with tension. He struggled and appeared to be second-guessing something in God's plan for his final battle—death.

Before Jesus would take up his cross, he invited people to follow him, and many did. Everyone is hungry for answers. We need our lives to make sense, and we have an emptiness in our hearts and minds that needs to be filled. That craving for emotional and intellectual fulfillment can only be satisfied by taking the same spiritual path Jesus took. He warned that it will not be easy; the journey will have peaks and valleys. At times, your life will be sky-high, filled with God's blessings, but there will also be troubled times when you hit bottom with no earthly way out. One of the secrets to survival is found in the Lord's Prayer. We are to ask God, "Give us this day our daily bread" (Matthew 6:11). God knows all about providing us with our physical and mental needs. He cares about us and has good things in store for us.

For the doubters who followed him, Jesus used his powers to do great things that shocked their hearts and minds. For the people seeking a follow-your-heart moment, he miraculously healed the sick, the blind, and the lame. For the analytical thinkers, he did amazing things that defied the laws of logic. He turned large storage jars of water into wine. He fed 5,000 people with only five loaves of barley and two small fish. Jesus also rebuked a devastating storm on the Sea of Galilee and walked on water. These stories have influenced followers for a lifetime, yet at the time, it was only a preview of God's greater plan.

Then, in the final days of his ministry, Jesus became the sacrificial lamb who would feed both the heart and the mind. When that time arrived, we find Jesus mentally preparing for the ultimate test of his faith—to give his life as a ransom for ours. There would be not only physical pain but spiritual consequences. Jesus would restore our relationship with God by taking on the weight of the world's sins.

In the Garden of Gethsemane, Jesus knew that God's plan for his death was about to become a reality, and needed to mentally prepare for the upcoming chain of events. He prayed a passionate prayer before Judas betrayed him and his disciples abandoned him.

> ***Jesus went out as usual to the Mount of Olives, and his disciples followed him. On reaching the place, he said to them, "Pray that you will not fall into temptation." He withdrew about a stone's throw beyond them, knelt down and prayed, "Father, if you are willing, take this cup from me; yet not my will, but yours be done." An angel from***

***heaven appeared to him and strengthened him. And being in anguish, he prayed more earnestly, and his sweat was like drops of blood falling to the ground.***

Luke 22:39-44

The path Jesus took from that point was brutal. As the Son of God, he knew all the details of the next 24 hours. He knew he would be mocked, spit upon, falsely accused, and beaten with whips that would shred his back to the bone. This was just the start of the misery he would endure before facing a slow painful suffocation on the ultimate torture device—the cross.

Before we look at how Jesus used this time in the garden to mentally prepare for his final battle, some questions may never be answered. Why are we privy to only one sentence of his passionate prayer and left to speculate what else he said? And what did the cup represent that Jesus found so disheartening?

Instead of diving into a deep theological debate to determine the contents of the cup, my perspective skims the surface. Jesus used the expression "drinking from the cup" several times as if it were a common phrase associated with the crucifixion. Jesus even confirmed that his disciples James and John would drink from his cup at their own deaths (Matthew 20:23).

The only thing to drink after being nailed to the cross would be the tears flowing from the slow, painful torture, a process that might last for days. Having a cup associated with a crucifixion probably originated from Psalm 80:5, "You have fed them with the bread of tears; you have made them drink tears by the bowlful," or from Psalms 42:3, "My tears have been my food day and night, while people say to me all day long, 'Where is your God?'" When the tears stop flowing, and the cup is empty, it's safe to say the end of a life is near.

## Chapter 12

While Jesus was in the garden reviewing his Father's plan, the tears in the cup were not his own. Jesus had felt his Father's love and was now faced with his Father's sorrow. A father's agony of seeing his son cry out in pain while suffering unjustly would be almost as great as the actual experience. Jesus would have to endure images of both. To make matters worse, God as his Father was not only responsible for planning his horrible death but had the power to save him—but didn't.

When Jesus told his disciples "My soul is overwhelmed with sorrow to the point of death" (Matthew 26:38), it was because "I and the Father are one" (John 10:30). His soul was hard-wired with a direct line to God. No wonder he wanted the cup to pass. His Father's tears over the upcoming crucifixion were too overwhelming for his humanity.

The events that followed would require Jesus to face his accusers. To show up with overwhelming sorrow would not be an appropriate appearance for the Son of God. He would need to be "in the moment," mentally pliable to offer an appropriate response to any situation. To do so, his mental warehouse would need extensive remodeling.

God provided the tools for the transformation by dispatching an angel to "strengthen him"—by turbo-charging his power-sword. God's love would restore his troubled heart, mind, and soul, but his mental inventory was still a mess. Everything tagged with negative emotion had to go. He would have to "demolish arguments" and "take captive every thought" that stands in the way of God's will.

This meant spiritual warfare was taking place in the theater of his mind, and Jesus fought like never before. His divine connection had changed the momentum at his military base of operations. The fortitude to stand strong and fight back against his future accusers became so intense that his aggressive sweat was tinged with blood.

As it turns out, some people do sweat blood. It is a rare medical condition called hematohidrosis. This condition happens when extreme stress causes the blood capillaries near the skin to rupture, and the blood leaks into the sweat glands.

After Jesus completed the transformation at his military base of operations, look at how he faced the large crowd armed with swords and clubs sent to seize him.

> ***Jesus, knowing all that was going to happen to him, went out and asked them, "Who is it you want?***
>
> ***"Jesus of Nazareth," they replied.***
>
> ***"I am he," Jesus said. (And Judas the traitor was standing there with them.) When Jesus said, "I am he," they drew back and fell to the ground.***
>
> John 18:4-6

This was not the Jesus they expected. His powerful words carried the type of authority and courage that caught them off-balance. His fear of facing any confrontation had been annihilated by a triple-edged sword of confidence forged from power, love, and self-discipline (2 Timothy 1:7).

## God's Big Picture

Everything God does is an expression of love. God wants to connect with you and establish a loving relationship that will last for all eternity. Jesus was sent to make that spiritual connection happen.

> ***For God so loved the world that he gave his one and only Son, that whoever believes in him shall not perish but have eternal life.***

## Chapter 12

John 3:16

Jesus often talked with his disciples about God's future plans. He would express the love God felt for them and repeatedly warned them of his crucifixion. With all the distractions that came with Jesus' popularity, none of it seemed to sink in. They didn't realize how their lives would drastically change because of Jesus' death and resurrection. Jesus said:

> ***"Nevertheless, I tell you the truth: it is to your advantage that I go away, for if I do not go away, the Helper will not come to you. But if I go, I will send him to you."***
>
> John 16:7 (ESV)

God's master plan is for you to have a full-time helper or advocate—the Holy Spirit. Think of him as an assistant coach who can gain access to the head coach—God. Jesus fulfilled God's plan so that you can experience the type of relationship he enjoys with God. That relationship leads to contentment and an abundant life as well as eternal life with him.

Your body is a temple, and Jesus died for you so he can move in. He is willing to be your full-time coach and has the counseling skills to bring your heart, mind, and soul together in a unified collaboration. Before that can happen, the current temple inventory must be cleaned up. Everything God finds unacceptable must be removed. Starting fresh is a part of the process Jesus described as being "born again." But don't think you can do it on your own. You can't. You must ask for divine power. You can make it a simple prayer of acceptance. Just ask Jesus to come into your life and to forgive the mess (sins that keep you from having a relationship with God). When you acknowledge the power of the cross and accept God's loving ability (grace) to forgive sin, Jesus will become your Lord and Savior. He has promised to help you to live a better life when you continue to pursue the heart and mind of Jesus.

## It's Not Game-Over!

Dying on the cross and conquering death was not the final chapter for Jesus. In due time, he will leave Heaven to finish his mission. However, this Jesus is different, unrecognizable because he will return as a Warrior-Messiah-King. You won't find a portrait of this Jesus in any contemporary church. He will be wearing his warrior face with eyes "like blazing fire" and a robe dipped in blood and have tattoos on his thigh. He will be riding a white horse and leading the armies of Heaven into war. The Apostle John writes this about the end times in the book of Revelation:

> ***I saw heaven standing open and there before me was a white horse, whose rider is called Faithful and True. With justice he judges and wages war. His eyes are like blazing fire, and on his head are many crowns. He has a name written on him that no one knows but he himself. He is dressed in a robe dipped in blood, and his name is the Word of God. The armies of heaven were following him, riding on white horses and dressed in fine linen, white and clean. Coming out of his mouth is a sharp sword with which to strike down the nations. "He will rule them with an iron scepter." He treads the winepress of the fury of the***

***wrath of God Almighty. On his robe and on his thigh he has this name written:***

***KING OF KINGS AND LORD OF LORDS.***

Revelation 19:11-16

Why would anyone go against the wrath of Jesus, especially when his strategy calls for striking down the nations with a "sharp sword" and ruling with an "iron scepter"? Why not join the winning side? Enlist in the army of the living God. The deadline for open enrollment may end sooner than you think. Once the gates of Heaven open up and you see Jesus riding a "white horse," it might be too late to sign up.

Why hold back when there is so much to gain? Your boot camp experience won't be that bad. Not when Jesus is with you. As your faith grows, Jesus has the authority, as Commander in Chief, to grant full access to all the weapons in *God's Sports Arsenal*.

# DISCUSSION QUESTIONS

DISCUSSION QUESTIONS

# GAME WITHIN THE GAME CHAPTER 1

1. How has "luck" influenced your behavior? Do you have any special routines or articles of clothing that inspire confidence before a game or special event? If you have decided to play a "game within the game," how has your perspective on the power of luck changed?

2. What is your definition of weaponizing your thoughts? Do you agree with the biblical perspective that aims at changing hearts and minds? What motivates you? Does it take a great story or a list of facts to provide game-time inspiration? Elaborate.

3. Read the Greatest Commandment in Mark 12:30. List the three entities and how they relate to your strengths. Which ones do you need to improve to transform your life and achieve greatness?

4. When it comes to the head and the heart mindsets, which one is more dominant in your personality, and which one has its foot on the brake pedal when you are facing a new or tense situation?

5. The micro-soccer athletes were ready to break the "__________ ________ ___________ ________" sports rule and use hate as a pre-game motivator. Describe a situation where you lost your temper or patience and experienced pain and regrets. Besides sports, have you gone into a situation loaded for bear and found out your weaponized thoughts were not appropriate after hearing the whole story? Explain.

6. Read James 4:1. Can you apply this verse to situations in your life or a sports version of the heart and mind rivalry? Explain what it means to have "desires that battle within you."

7. With all the celebrating after winning, it's easy to see the heart take control, but how do you feel after a tough loss ... not only in sports but in life as well? When mentally reviewing mistakes or dealing with faulty expectations, in what ways is your head placing blame? In what ways is your heart finding fault? In other words, explain whether it was a lack of emotional intensity or a failure in executing the game plan that has you upset.

8. The key to weaponizing your thoughts is to create powerful sports tags. To test your skill, pick one teammate (or friend) and print their name below. List all the logical information about that person. These tags should read like a sports resumé or include other admirable skills. Then write down the emotional characteristics that best define that person and what effect they have on you and your teammates or friends.

Name ________________________________________

Logical tags

Emotional tags

Congratulations! You just created your first weapon or card of confidence. Now upgrade it to a weapon of verbal confidence by writing down a humorous introductory one-liner as in the social experiment exercise.

# DISCUSSION QUESTIONS

## SPORTS WAREHOUSE CHAPTER 2

1. Have you ever played for or supported a team that was blown-out? Describe those feelings of defeat. How long did they last? Did it take a day or week before time healed those wounds or did something positive happen to replace the feelings of disappointment? Explain.

2. Read Luke 6:43-45. Jesus is talking about your heart being a mental warehouse. What does it mean to produce and store-up "good fruit?" Does this teaching give you a discriminating appetite for "good fruit" and a desire to toss out the "bad fruit?" How can you apply Jesus's teaching to your situation?

3. The prime directive of sports is to mentally organize what you need to execute, and it all takes place inside your sports warehouse. In what ways will these concepts change your approach to mental preparedness for sports and in your personal life?

4. Building a large mental inventory of "good things" requires the approval of your head and heart. List some of the "good things" in sports and in your personal life that draws you in and captivates your heart and mind.

**5. Paul writes a bold statement in 1 Corinthians 9:25: "Every athlete exercises self-control in all things." (ESV) Do you agree that self-discipline is a huge part of the game and in the game of life? List areas where your game is strong and where more self-control is needed.**

**6. How would you define the expression, "He (or she) plays with the heart of a warrior"? In what ways does the concept of your head and heart working inside the sports warehouse apply to this expression? How can you use this information to build or maintain your confidence?**

**7. King Solomon emphasizes using the heart as a long-term storage device and keeping it well-guarded. Which commands would you store up and how can you protect them? The same concept can be applied to set up short and long-term goals. How can you keep outside influences from stealing your hopes and dreams?**

**8. How do you feel about being blessed with a hunter's heart? How has your sense of adventure led you to some exhilarating moments?**

**9. Have you or someone you know experienced being in "hunting mode"? Has the need to put someone on your radar happened outside of competitive sports? Explain the attraction; was it in a positive or a negative way?**

# DISCUSSION QUESTIONS

# MILITARY BASE OF OPERATIONS CHAPTER 3

1. If this is your first small group experience, it may be hard to open up about past mistakes, but spiritual growth involves admitting we are not perfect people. What lingering mistakes in sports or in life are you keeping secret, even though they should be old news?

2. Is the concept of having a military base of operations difficult for you to grasp? Which building do you accept or reject and why?

3. Are you in charge of your military base of operations, or is it in charge of you? Share a time when you let your guard down and let some of the "bad things" (hate, greed, envy) escape from your mental warehouse. How much damage control was needed to repair the inappropriate behavior?

4. The Strategic Command Center houses the theater of your mind. How often do you stop and use it to play out future scenarios? It's our nature to expect the worst, so how can we turn that around and see a positive future?

5. The military base is designed to protect your temple from spiritual warfare. Find and share some verses where the Bible states your body is a temple. (Hint: start with 1 Corinthians 3)

**6. Is there something you hate about practice or something at school or work that really bugs you? Do some drama replacement therapy by writing down the details of your frustration. What steps can you take to replace the emotional tag with something more tolerable or more productive? If the emotional tag is too big to handle, how can God help you deal with it?**

**7. In Philippians 4:8 the Apostle Paul writes a list of "whatever is" things to store up in your mental inventory. Has this changed your perspective on how to process your surroundings to store up a positive attitude? How can you trigger a reminder to practice what Paul preaches?**

**8. Have you experienced a "turbo-boost moment" where everything seemed to happen in slow motion? Was it in sports or some other type of situation (such as an accident)?**

**9. Do you need to organize your sports warehouse before every play or does your pre-game program set the tone for the entire game? In either case, explain the process that works for you.**

**10. Do you let your heart celebrate big time after a significant event? In what ways does it show?**

## DISCUSSION QUESTIONS

# SPORTS ARMORY - WEAPONS OF EMOTION CHAPTER 4

1. Read the story of David and Goliath in 1 Samuel 17. Why do you think God wanted this story in the Bible? What stands out and how does it excite your heart or your mind or both?

2. Everyone has faced a Goliath-sized problem. Can you think of a previous battle where your heart overruled the risk factor, and you pulled a tiger by the tail anyway? Did you end up with the attitude of I'm never doing that again or did the experience build your confidence? Share your story.

3. Have you noticed that most leaders have a contagious confidence that infects everyone around them? Do you depend on someone else to step forward and be the leader or are you working toward filling those shoes? What steps can you take to build a better weapon of confidence and keep your head or heart strong?

4. What will it take for you to become aggressive in sports without crossing the line? In what ways can you control your aggressiveness when not playing sports?

5. Possessiveness can be a powerful weapon. Have you felt this type of emotion during a game? If so, how well did you utilize its power? Has this possessive attitude surfaced as a protective attitude in other areas of your life, such as in protecting someone from harm? Elaborate.

6. A sports tattoo creates a unique emotional attachment to a prized possession. Look at the stories behind some of your past prized possessions that may or may not be sports related. Can you break down the unique bond into areas of emotion and logic? How can you apply a meaningful sports tattoo to your next game?

7. God's goal is to help you develop perseverance so you can be mature enough to face any combat situation. This means your arsenal should have the right weapons to get the job done. Which weapons of emotion will you need to conquer your next set of challenging situations?

8. Do you remember the guidelines for filling the sports warehouse? List the top three rules of sports warfare from the previous chapter.

(1)

(2)

(3)

## DISCUSSION QUESTIONS

## GOD'S BOOT CAMP CHAPTER 5

1. Every great athlete goes through some type of learning curve. During training, failure can be a cruel teacher. Can you think of a time when you didn't have the proper training and had to fly by the seat of your pants? What was the outcome?

2. What you say will be remembered longer than what you think. Read Joshua 1:9 out loud with a powerful voice. Would this battle cry motivate you to step out of your comfort zone? Explain why we as soldiers need to hear these words of encouragement and when it is appropriate to use this verse.

3. When you look at the past, present, and future of your life, are you still going through a boot camp experience? It's all part of God's plan, so explain your present mission.

4. Have you faced any roaring lions? Who or what obstacle is standing in your way and keeping you from completing your mission? What are some of your favorite bible verses that will overcome your current circumstances?

**5. Have you ever thought of God as a warrior? List all four faces of God. Which of the four faces do you wear the most and when do you wear it?**

**(1)**

**(2)**

**(3)**

**(4)**

**6. Have you ever lost your confidence during a game or in a real-life situation? Was it your nerves or lack of sports skills that got the best of you? Who is looking to steal your confidence or what type of situation would make you throw it away?**

**7. Winning is all about having the right weapons. Read about God's private arsenal in Jeremiah 50:25. Use the index in the back of your Bible or the search tool on a Bible website to find more weapons in God's arsenal. List your favorite weapons.**

**(1)**

**(2)**

**(3)**

**8. There is a shortage of inspiring leaders in every walk of life. How can you improve your leadership skills and step up to be an influential leader in sports and at home, church, school, or work? Share your thoughts on any personal leadership goals or previous leadership seminars you have attended.**

## DISCUSSION QUESTIONS

## GOD'S SPORTS ARSENAL CHAPTER 6

**1. List all the components in the armor of God. Other than the sword of the Spirit, which one appeals to you and why?**

**2. How thick is your "shield of faith"? Presently, are you being hit by "flaming arrows"? How many can you extinguish before there's serious damage, and how quickly do you recover from a fiery confrontation?**

**3. The sword of the Spirit is God's word, but not all the verses in the Bible make good swords. Do you have a meaningful Bible verse that would make a good sword? Identify the three biblical swords and the components of the triple-edged sword in this chapter. Which sword would you hold on to during a game and which one would you still use when the season is over?**

**4. Self-confidence is a very important attribute to have in sports and in life. Confidence can be gained from reviewing past battle experiences or built from mentally organizing future sports tags. When forging your "sword of confidence," which process do you prefer, and in what situations do you need a bigger sword? Elaborate.**

**5. See if you can add the "sword of" phrase to Hebrews 10:35 and memorize this verse. Define some of the ways you can become "richly rewarded"?**

**6. Read Matthew 5:14-16. Do you see yourself as a "light of the world"? If yes, why? If not, how can you charge up your batteries and shine a bright light on those around you?**

**7. Use a Bible search tool to find out more about the Ark of the Covenant. Search for other weapons as well and write down several favorites.**

**8. Everyone says, "Have a good day," when they should be saying, "Make it a great day." Have you ever prayed for wisdom before starting the day or just when a conflict arises? In either case, what was the result?**

## DISCUSSION QUESTIONS

## EXTREME MENTAL GAMES CHAPTER 7

1. When it comes to extreme pre-game rituals, only Michael Jordan could pull off eating a 23-ounce steak and wearing his lucky shorts under his game uniform. How about your game-day rituals? Do you have special food, drink, or clothing that provides emotional support? Share your favorite comfort food.

2. Before a major event, do you need to take a time-out to clear your head, or will your competitive heart not let you sit still? Which one causes you the most grief?

3. Repetition is an important part of learning. How many times do you need to practice something before it fills your sports warehouse and you can say, "I got this"?

4. What is your definition of muscle control and how does it relate to being in the zone? Which muscle control apps are running right now and which ones are needed to make big plays during a game?

**5. Do you know of other athletes who control their breathing when competing? Have you controlled your breathing in sports or some other type of exercise? If so, share your experience and the results.**

**6. Visualizing future game situations is an important skill and not just in sports. How much time do you spend in the theater of your mind planning upcoming events? What areas of preparation do you focus on?**

**7. Sports tattoos are very powerful weapons. Explain how your favorite sports tattoo can be used to maintain a "combat mode" attitude.**

**8. The laser-target-lock tattoo is adaptable to any sport. Explain each of its components and how it affects the other buildings in your military base of operation.**

**9. The secret to making a powerful sports tattoo is to create an image that enhances fundamental skills with weaponized emotions. What areas of your game do you need to improve and what type of image would work?**

DISCUSSION QUESTIONS

# DISARMING PERFORMANCE ANXIETY
# CHAPTER 8

1. Have you seen someone blow up with extreme emotion which ended a long-term relationship at work or in school? Was it over some little thing? Explain what Jesus meant in Luke 6:46 when he said, "For the mouth speaks what the heart is full of" and how a little thing can trigger an emotional explosion.

2. Take time to assess your current state of anxiety. Are you overwhelmed and often experience a nervous sweat or extreme butterflies? Or are you feeling fairly normal? Regardless, what is on your list of insurmountable fears?

3. Anxiety can be defined as being pulled in different directions. Explain a frequent conflict in your life and how you were caught up in the mess. Explain the effect on your head and heart and how you can deal with the source of the anxiety.

4. Read 1 Peter 5:7. When it comes to anxiety retention, most people have an all-you-can-eat buffet of negativity. Why do they fill their plate but won't share their grief with God?

**5. Read Philippians 4:8. The Apostle Paul recommends a list of "whatever is" things to maintain a healthy mental warehouse. What are some of the ways you can toss out the "bad things" to make room for a positive attitude?**

**6. What is holding you back? Have your past mistakes on the field or in everyday life become stumbling blocks? Identify and address the strongholds that are at work in your life. What is your demolition plan to get rid of them? And what are you hiding from God inside your stronghold?**

**7. Have you experienced tossing and turning before a major event? How will you wage war to turn the tide and what weapons will you use that are not of this world? Will you seek God's help and how can he help you?**

**8. Read Romans 12:2. In this fast-paced world we are expected to squeeze more and more out of every day. But Paul writes that less is more, so we should renovate our minds. Have you set aside time to unload and refurbish your mental warehouse? How can you make room to explore God's will for your life? If you have figured out how to renew your mind, share your experience and the results.**

DISCUSSION QUESTIONS

## GOD'S TIME-OUT CHAPTER 9

1. One of the habits of highly successful people is that they meditate as part of a daily routine. Have you taken a time-out during a busy day to close your eyes and be with God for more than a few minutes? How often do you plug into God's dynamic power for a spiritual tune-up and what were the results?

2. Read Romans 12:15-16. What does it mean to be "in the moment"? How does God's version of being "in the moment" compare with Phil Jackson's version? Have you ever experienced that feeling? Describe the situation and how often it has happened.

3. Do you agree or disagree that the "heart is deceitful above all things"? Name a time when you have felt internal tension between your head and your heart, and how did you deal with it?

**4. Read Proverbs 4:23. What does it mean to guard your heart? How can you follow through on that command?**

**5. Read Acts 4:32. Do you have a similar heart and mind as some of your friends or teammates? In what areas do you connect with that person(s)?**

**6. Become intentional about meditating with God. Find that quiet place where you can spend some heavenly time alone with God. Focus on unloading any negative inventory in your mental warehouse and keep a record of the effects.**

DISCUSSION QUESTIONS

## THE MICRO-WARRIOR CHAPTER 10

1. What are you passionate about? Explain what it is that excites and motivates you to invest time and/or money.

2. How would you define your micro-sports buddy? How does it compare with Paul's version in Ephesians 1:18, or with Peter's version in 1 Peter 3:4?

3. Read Proverbs 4:23. Why do you need to guard your micro-warrior? Read Matthew 15:19. Assess your own micro-warrior. How can you rein him or her in and stay focused on your goals and dreams?

4. Are you convinced that simple mental games can be used as a distraction before games? What are you or other athletes you know using to make the time fly by?

**5. In what ways is your micro-warrior a gift or a curse? What improvements can you make to be more productive?**

**6. Using a muscle car as a sports tattoo works well for sports like football or soccer, but it would sink a swimmer. Name some other sports where an adrenalin sports tattoo can improve performance and how it must be adapted to motivate your micro-warrior.**

**7. Are you ready to join the "armies of the living God"? In what ways can you defend God's kingdom?**

## DISCUSSION QUESTIONS

# GREATEST COMMANDMENTS IN SPORTS
# CHAPTER 11

1. Read Mark 12:30. Think about the greatest accomplishments in your life. How did it take the power of both your head and your heart to achieve them? Was there also a soul connection?

2. In the first chapter, you were asked to write down whether your head or heart was holding you back. Has your perspective changed? Explain your present position and what changes, if any, will improve your mental game.

3. Read Galatians 5:14 and James 2:8. Why would God want this commandment to be such a high priority, and how can you become a better Good Samaritan? Have you been convicted of missed opportunities to use this commandment? Share some of those missed situations and the reason your head or heart was holding you back.

4. Why would the second commandment say that loving your neighbor is just as important as loving yourself? In what ways can you love yourself? Explain how these principles can apply to sports.

**5. Read Matthew 7:13-14. Are you able to find and stay on the narrow road? Is it your head, heart, or soul that tends to lead you astray? Do you have, or are you thinking of having, an accountability partner? In other words, a go-to guy other than a spouse or parent you can trust with your fears and failures without any repercussions. What steps can you take to build this type of relationship?**

**6. Read 1 Corinthians 16:14. How can you apply this verse to every part of your personal life and make it happen?**

**7. How can you anchor your sports warehouse to withstand stormy weather? What are some of the ways you can clean it up to make room for God's perspective and his plans for your life?**

**8. How can you apply the greatest commandment to your sports life and keep track of its application?**

## DISCUSSION QUESTIONS

## THE FINAL BATTLE CHAPTER 12

1. When you look at all the things that Jesus did during his ministry, what stands out? In what ways did Jesus appeal to your head and your heart? Was there a teaching or story about Jesus that reached you spiritually right down to your soul?

2. There are numerous interpretations of the contents of the cup at the Garden of Gethsemane. What is your perspective?

3. The death of a close friend or relative can be an extremely emotional event. How would you mentally prepare for it?

4. Read Matthew 4:1-11 and Luke 22:43. Compare the personal involvement the angels had with Jesus. Do you believe angels are watching over you and waiting to help you? Have you gone through a tough time and awakened the next day feeling great? Was it more than getting a good night's sleep that changed your attitude?

**5. In John 16:7 the English Standard Version (ESV) designates the Holy Spirit as the "helper." Other versions of the Bible describe the Holy Spirit as a "friend, counselor, advocate, or comforter." Which of these five interpretations would you choose and how could it best meet your needs?**

**6. Your body is a temple, designed to house the Holy Spirit. If we are to experience spiritual growth and expand God's kingdom, the Holy Spirit will need to be protected by your military base of operations. Why does it need spiritual food and protection? (Hint: Use a Bible study tool to search for "living water" and "bread of life.")**

**7. Read Revelation 19:11-16. Have you heard this perspective of Jesus before? How does it impact your previous ideas of who he is?**

**8. Most of us have built a comfort zone. Is there someone or something motivating you to step out and enlist in God's armed forces? Who or what might that be?**

## Notes and idea page

www.ingramcontent.com/pod-product-compliance
Lightning Source LLC
LaVergne TN
LVHW051506080426
835509LV00017B/1937